THE AMAZING LIFE OF JOHN COOPER FITCH
An American Hero
By Art Evans

THE AMAZING LIFE OF JOHN COOPER FITCH

By Art Evans

FIRST EDITION

Library of Congress Card Catalog Number: LC 2014 937858

ISBN 1-58388-329-0/978-1-58388-329-7

Published by Enthusiast Books
1830A Hanley Road
Hudson, WI 54016
Phone: 715-381-9755, Fax 715-381-9756
Email: info@enthusiastbooks.com
www.enthusiastbooks.com

The quote on the cover was made by Carroll Shelby. He had been able to go over much of the text before his death. Photos from the John Fitch archive maintained by Bob Sirna, the Daimler Benz archive, the General Motors archive through the courtesy of Bob Lutz, the Art Evans archive and the Jim Gessner collection. Photos by Bernard Cahier, Lester Nehamkin, Bob Trolone, Allen Kuhn, Brian Stevens, Steve Johnson and Jim Sitz.

INTRODUCTION

If someone were to write a novel about the life of John Fitch, it would seem so far-fetched as to be virtually unbelievable. John sailed the Gulf of Mexico patrolling for German subs on the eve of WWII. He was a WWII hero, the boyfriend of Kathleen Kennedy and buddy of JFK, won the first GP of Argentina and was kissed by Evita Peron, was the first SCCA National Champion, a member of the 1955 World Championship Mercedes Benz team, part of the all-conquering Cunningham team, credited with transforming Corvettes into genuine sports cars, designed the safe and challenging Lime Rock racecourse, created the Corvair Sprint and invented Fitch Inertial Barriers, those barrels seen on our freeways and highways that have saved countless lives. Wow! These are just a few highlights of his incredible life.

I was privileged to have John Fitch as a close friend for many years. I ran across him in 1953 when he won the main event of the SCCA National Race at March Air Force Base. But we didn't become friends until 1965 when he came to California to appear in a commercial. I was the cinematographer. At the time I had a 30-foot sailboat, and since John was an avid rag sailor, I invited him aboard. We sailed out of King Harbor in Redondo Beach, where I had a slip. Afterwards, whenever John came to California, we went sailing. From then on our friendship developed over the years.

John Fitch died peacefully at age 95 on October 31, 2012 at his home in Lakeville, Connecticut. As always, he was in my mind and still is. Over the years I talked with John about various aspects of his life experiences. Eventually, a number of things came to light that have not been previously published nor well known. Some of what I have written here is at odds with accounts in other books and/or articles. One reason John told me is that he didn't want his wife, Elizabeth, to know about certain factors about his life. After Elizabeth's death, he told me I could go ahead. Before his marriage, Fitch had been quite the ladies man and he didn't want Elizabeth to know about it. After meeting Elizabeth, she was his "one and only" for the balance of their lives.

THE BEGINNINGS

John sprang from an interesting ancestry. John's great-great-great grandfather and namesake (1743-1798) was a lieutenant in the fledgling U.S. Navy. In June, 1785, Lt. Fitch put a steamboat he had invented into the water near Davisville, Pennsylvania. The next year he tested it on the Delaware River. At the time, our constitution was being written in Philadelphia. So he took a few of its framers out for a cruise. In 1790, Fitch put together a second steamboat that transported freight as well as passengers on the Delaware for a time. Congress issued a patent to Fitch. It was signed by George Washington and dated August 26, 1791. Another patent for the invention was issued by the King of France. But, as all schoolchildren know, Robert Fulton invented the steamboat. Right? No, wrong. Perhaps someday our history textbooks will relate the actual facts.   Below: The John Fitch steamboat.

In the nineteenth century, the Fitch family moved to Indianapolis. In 1875, John's grandfather started a chewing gum factory where he made Fitch's Spearmint Pepsin gum as well as Resto-Curo gum, which was claimed to cure the tobacco habit. In addition, it was supposed to "restore impotent men to manly vigor." Unable to compete with Wrigley, the company didn't survive.

John's father, Robert Vanderbilt Fitch, was a contractor who built houses in Indianapolis. But in remembrance of his great-great grandfather, he is credited with building the first closed body on a horseless carriage as well as a paddle-wheel steamboat. He launched it on the White River where, unfortunately, it sank. John Cooper Fitch was born on August 4, 1917 in Indianapolis, Indiana. John's father and mother were divorced in 1923 when John was 6 years old.

The following year John's mother married George Spindler, a sales executive for the Stutz Motor Company. (A Stutz Bearcat raced in the first Indy 500.) George himself raced a Stutz there one time, but didn't finish among the leaders. During John's growing-up years, Spindler took him for many tours of the brickyard during testing or when demonstrating new models. Fitch recalled "hanging on with everything I had" to the seat of a thundering Stutz Bearcat during a record run. His stepfather believed that speed and performance were important for sales, a lesson John later took to heart. The 500 was a very special event for the city then—as it is now—and young John attended every year until he went away to school.

One time the famous French race driver, Louis Chiron, came to visit and stayed with the Spindler family while he was attending the Indy 500. John never forgot meeting Chiron. He was John's childhood hero. In 1953, John would finish Le Mans ahead of Chiron.

When Fitch was 16, he went to high school at the Kentucky Military Institute in Louisville. The school had classes in Florida for the winter semester where the Institute had acquired several hotels that had gone broke due to the depression. John found an old Chrysler that had been abandoned on the beach. He, with the help of two classmates, put the car together and got it running. When the winter term was over, he drove it to Louisville. The problem was the brakes were no good, so John had some hairy moments crossing the mountains.   Below: John's backyard special.

John's grades were generally okay, but in his final high school year, his algebra teacher told him he was failing in the subject and wouldn't graduate. John knew that the teacher was in the process of building a trailer and needed a chassis. So John offered his Chrysler for that purpose and, lo-and-behold, passed algebra and graduated. Next Fitch enrolled in Lehigh University at Bethlehem, Pennsylvania where, at the behest of his parents, he majored in civil engineering.

TRAVELS

Soon John acquired wanderlust. "I wanted to see the world," he said. Fortunately, he had a few dollars tucked away due to an inheritance from his grandfather. So after a year at Lehigh, he dropped out, bought an Indian Twin motorcycle and rode it to New Orleans. After enjoying the delights of that city, he traded the Indian to a seaman he had met in New Orleans for a Fiat Topolino. John found he loved driving the little car so much that he ended up driving it nonstop all the way to New York City.

Fitch had enjoyed his two small trips so much that he determined to continue. He decided he wanted to see Europe. His initial idea was to get a horse and ride it from London to Rome. He speculated that this would be an ideal way to not only see different countries, but also experience the culture and learn new languages.

In the spring of 1939, John sold his Fiat and booked passage on a Dutch freighter, the *Beemstrerdyke,* that was going to England. The ship was painfully slow and the trip took three weeks. When he got to London, he applied for a tourist visa for Europe, but none were being issued due to the impending hostilities there. So the horse plan fell by the wayside.

In the meantime, John had met a beautiful ballet dancer and they became an item. She introduced him to her acquaintance, Ham Johnson, who lived on a barge. Ham was part of a group of young people who lived on converted barges. Most were students (or had been) from Oxford or Cambridge and many were communists. John and Ham got along so Ham invited John to move in.

JOHN COOPER FITCH

Eventually John and Ham got tired of all the radical rant, so they decided to tour England, Scotland and Wales. They bought a used and somewhat tired MG Magnette for $700 and set out. While the engine and gearbox were fine, the suspension was miserable, the starter didn't work and it leaked oil.   Below: John and the MG.

Whenever they had to park, they would find a slope so they wouldn't have to push-start it. Their first stop was at the famous Brooklands race track near London. When they arrived, an event was underway and Fitch saw a road race with Prince Bira speeding around in an E.R.A. The experience, John would later recall, made a lasting impression.

Next they wended their way towards Scotland with Fitch taking photographs all along the way. When they got to York, about 150 miles north of London, they were arrested and put in jail. The police had seen John taking pictures of the countryside with some military vehicles in the background. They suspected the young men might be spies. They had to remain in jail until the film was developed, showing they were just tourists.

When they were driving through Wales and John was at the wheel, he got into a short dice with a BMW 328, perhaps the best sports car of the time. In comparison with the BMW, the MG was sadly outclassed and John was impressed when it rapidly left them in the dust.

A teen-aged Stirling Moss competing at a hill climb in England at the wheel of a BMW 328.

BACK TO THE U.S.

But then their trip was rudely interrupted. On September 1, 1939, Germany invaded Poland and, three days later, England, allied with Poland at the time, declared war on Germany. Fitch tried to join the Royal Air Force Eagle Squadron of American volunteers, but was turned down because England then had all the pilots it needed. So John sold his half of the MG to Ham and returned to the U.S.

Below: John's schooner, the "Banshee."

John ended up in Sarasota, Florida where he found a 32-foot sailboat for which he paid $1,500 with money from his inheritance. He named his boat "Banshee." The Coast Guard was hold-

ing courses for volunteers to participate in its antisubmarine pa-
trols, so John enrolled and learned some basic navigation including
how to take star sightings with a sextant.

With war looming, Fitch and his first mate (above), a
girlfriend named Tina he had met before going to England, sailed
in and around the Gulf of Mexico for 12 months or so, looking for,
but never finding any German subs. Eventually, they headed along
the coast towards New Orleans.

THE WAR

By 1941, it was obvious that America would become more involved in the war, so John sold his boat in New Orleans to a German immigrant named Karl Baskel. Leaving his girlfriend, John enlisted in the Army on April 29, 1941. After basic training and primary flight training at Lakeland, Florida, he was sent for advanced flight training at Turner Air Base, Georgia (where he would race some years later). While there, John became involved with the author, Carson McCullers, who had just been divorced and had come home to Columbus, Georgia.

 They met in October 1941. Carson's first book, *The Heart is a Lonely Hunter*, had been published the previous year and was a major success. McCullers (left) was working on another novel—*Reflections in a Golden Eye*—set on a military base. She was interested in John's training experiences and one time he even took her for a flight.

On Sunday, December 7, John was on leave and attending the Army-Navy game in Philadelphia with his stepfather. When the game was over it was announced that the Japanese had bombed Pearl Harbor. Everyone in uniform was ordered to report immediately to his or her unit. On December 12, John received his wings and was sent to Fort Dix, New Jersey where he patrolled the coastline near New York City, flying out of Ft. Dix.

In early 1942, John's squadron, the 15th Bombardment Light, was sent to England. It was the first American unit to arrive in Europe. The personnel had been flown, but the planes were loaded on a ship. The aircraft had been mistakenly sent to Russia. So A-20 Havocs were borrowed from the RAF. The first American engagement in the European theatre was a bombing raid on occupied France. Ironi-

cally, the date was July 4. All in all, John flew more than 50 missions to bomb targets over Western Europe during that year.

Some pilots and crew of the 15th. Fitch is on the left.

In the fall, the 15th was sent to Algeria to support the North African campaign. They harassed German armor and supply depots while dicing with Focke-Wulf 190 fighters.

JOHN COOPER FITCH

After the German occupation of Sicily and Italy, Fitch got the idea that it would be advantageous for American pilots to have some practice in shooting down German planes. So General Jimmy Doolittle ordered Fitch to organize a unit to fly captured German aircraft for training purposes. While flying a Messerschmitt 110 twin-engine fighter from Naples to Algeria, John was hit by American ground fire. When the landing gear failed to function, he had to crash land. Luckily, he was able to walk away.

Fitch after crash-landing the Messerschmitt 110.

After his North Africa tour, Fitch was sent to Wright Field (now Wright-Patterson Air Force Base) to serve as a test pilot. His first job was testing a B-25 that had been converted into what was hoped would be a tank killer. A 75mm canon (without the caisson) had been fitted with a recoil device and installed onto the aircraft. The pilot was the aimer. The idea was to point the plane at a tank and fire the canon. Floating targets were placed in nearby Lake Erie where John flew and fired until the device was perfected. Subsequently, 75mm canon-mounted B-25s were employed in the Pacific Theatre.

His next assignment was testing the maximum speed possible of a P-51 Mustang. When flown at full throttle, their engines had been failing due to overheating. So a water injection device was installed. John's task was to test the new device and fly at 35,000 feet with full throttle until the engine blew. Then he had to make a "dead stick" landing. He kept at this until the device was fully developed.

While at Wright Field, John was reunited with his sailboat girlfriend and, although unmarried, they lived together for a time. Interestingly enough, some others who would later become friends were also at Wright Field including two other pilots, Rodger Ward and Sam Hanks. Sam met his future wife, Alice, there. She was a civilian employee.

As an aside, future racing friends were also at Wright Field at one time or another including Sam Hanks and Carroll Shelby. They never met each other then.

After returning to the European Theatre, John was assigned to the Fourth Fighter Group, 335th Fighter Squadron, previously known as the "Eagle Squadron." Below: 335th pilots, Fitch on the left.

JOHN COOPER FITCH

He flew P-51s to escort bombers over Germany. During that time, John was one of the very few who shot down a Messerschmitt Me 262 jet, an almost impossible feat due to the jet's superior speed. He hit it while the jet was taking off. This was only the second time an American pilot was able to accomplish this extraordinary exploit.

By the end of 1944, there was no more Luftwaffe to threaten the bombers, so the fighters were redirected towards shooting at ground targets. In January 1945, John was trying to destroy a train engine near Nuremberg. He knew if he could hit the boiler, it would explode. On his first two passes, he missed. John realized that it would be dangerous to make a third pass because antiaircraft gunners could improve their aim. Even so, he made a third pass and was hit by antiaircraft fire and had to bail out. In his confusion, he bailed out on the wrong side of the plane. As he was pulling the ripcord, he was hit by the tail of the P-51 and injured. He broke his arm when he landed near the burning aircraft. Soon, members of the German "Home Guard" arrived with pitchforks and axes looking to kill the pilot. They were angry due to the constant bombing. John managed to hide under some nearby brush and eventually the Germans gave up the search. Later, while he was still hiding in the brush, some children came nearby to play. Fortunately, they didn't notice him.

John had a survival kit that included a compass, a cloth map, some food and other items. So when night came, he got up and started walking. The map indicated that France was some 200 miles away. Wearing his American flight suit, he knew he couldn't walk during daylight hours. So when dawn broke after the first day, he hid in the loft of a barn and went to sleep. The next morning, he was awakened by the farmer, who invited him into the farmhouse where the wife prepared breakfast for John. John gave some chocolate from his escape kit to the farmer's child.

TAKEN PRISONER

When it became known in the community that there was an American pilot at the farmhouse, John was taken to the nearby town of Altdorf near Nuremberg. The mayor—a Nazi—struck Fitch and threatened him with a knife. He wanted to kill him, but members of the city council objected. They knew that the war had been lost and didn't want to face any repercussions when the U.S. Army came. John was turned over to German military authorities.

Afterwards he was transported with some other prisoners through the city of Nuremberg, which had been heavily damaged and was still being bombed. The group with their guards were attacked by angry townspeople and narrowly escaped.

When Fitch arrived at Oberursel, an interrogation center, he was placed in solitary confinement and put on a starvation diet. During this time, he was questioned to find out if he had any information that might be useful. The sessions were lengthy and there were two interrogators, a "good guy" and a "bad guy," both of whom, of course, spoke fluent English. The bad guy was harsh, but there was no physical torture. After quite some time, the good guy revealed that he had lived in New Orleans, but that when the war started, he had returned to Germany to serve. It turned out the good guy had a close friend in New Orleans, one Karl Baskel, the same person to whom Fitch had sold his sailboat. After that, a sort of friendship developed between the interrogator and Fitch. This took place in February 1945. By then, it was obvious to everyone that Germany had lost the war. Eventually the good guy broke down, almost in tears, and confessed he had made a terrible mistake by returning to Germany. He had been happy and prosperous in New Orleans. He said that now all was lost; that he was ruined, as was Germany itself.

After the interrogation process, Fitch was moved to a prisoner-of-war camp about 150 miles from Oberursel. The train was continually bombed and strafed, so the trip took three days. Two weeks later, the prisoners were moved by foot 100 miles to a POW camp near the town of Moosburg, about 22 miles northeast of Munich. The long column of prisoners was strafed by allied planes and a number were killed.

The camp—Stalag VIIA—with 110,000 allied prisoners of war, was Germany's largest POW facility. The prisoners were cooped up in dirty, damp, dark and unheated barracks that were built to accommodate only 10,000. Large tents had been erected to house more. Frank Murphy, one of the American prisoners, described it: "Our cheerless barbed-wire encircled world was comprised exclusively of austere, dilapidated buildings, grungy tents, mud, and clusters of gaunt, emaciated men in shoddy, worn out clothing occupying every inch of space they could find." There wasn't enough food. Misery, diarrhea and dysentery were rampant.

In April, the Third Army was approaching. On April 26, American planes attacked targets in the nearby town of Moosburg and the prisoners could hear the sound of distant artillery. During the night of April 28, the Germans pulled out most of the guard force, leaving only a skeleton unit behind. The next day the remaining guards deserted their posts and turned their weapons over to their former prisoners.

When General Patton and his Army were about nine miles from Moosburg, he sent a staff car under a white flag requesting that the camp be surrendered without combat. The Colonel who commanded SS troops in Mossburg refused, so the Americans attacked. Following a short battle, the Germans retreated.

After what Fitch called a "wild ground fight during which a few of us were shot," the remaining guards fled. On April 29, the camp was liberated and General Patton arrived in his brightly-shined command car, decorated with sirens, spotlights and a four-star flag. After touring some of the camp, he got up on the hood of his car and spoke to a crowd of jubilant prisoners. Talking into a microphone attached to a loudspeaker on the car, he ordered the Nazi flag down and the American one raised. He said that "I'd like to stay with you awhile, but I have a date with a woman in Munich. It is 40 kilometers away and I've got to fight every damned inch of the way. God Bless you and thank you for what you have done."

Fitch hadn't taken a shower for months because there were no facilities for the prisoners. He and some others went to the guard's quarters to take showers. While there, Patton (right), wearing his notorious ivory-handled revolvers and highly-polished helmet liner, came in and personally greeted each stark-naked soldier. Finally, in his gritty, no nonsense manner, he said, "Well, now I have to go and kill some more Germans."

Eleven weeks after Fitch was shot down, he was flown to France on May 8, 1945. After stays in Paris and London, he sailed for home, arriving in August 1945. His war was over. (American GIs who had been prisoners or were injured were among the first be taken home.)

THE KENNEDY CONNECTION

Shortly after discharge, John bought a Taylorcraft float plane and flew around the country; even to the Bahamas. Finally he ended up in Florida and started a small charter service. Through a mutual friend, he was invited to a party at the Kennedy compound. He met Joe, Rose and their daughter, Kathleen (her nickname was "Kick"). They started to date. When Joe was the ambassador to the United Kingdom, Kathleen had met and married Lord Harrington. When her husband was killed in combat, she returned to the States to live with her parents.

John described Kathleen as tall and athletic. She had a sense of humor and was very perceptive regarding others' feelings. Still and all, as the daughter of the U.K. ambassador and widow of an English Lord, she was very much a part of what would later be called the "jet set."

John's dates with Kathleen included not only parties and dinners, but also less formal occasions such as fishing excursions. Kathleen took a photo of John and Rose, and then John took one of the two women. These pictures are now a part of the Fitch collection.

Fitch recalls Joe Kennedy as a rather crude individual who flaunted his much younger girlfriends in front of his family including Rose. John really liked Rose, who, he says, had a warm personality. He thought it took great fortitude to put up with Joe. But it was a Catholic marriage. In those days divorce wasn't contemplated.

John fishing with Rose Kennedy. Photo by Kathleen.

One particular party at the compound stuck in John's memory. There were a great many guests. Fitch remembered that Noel Coward and Jimmy Doolittle were there. Doolittle, of course, he had met during the war. John needed to relieve himself. Finding a long line at the inside facility, he repaired to a remote and secluded bush in the garden. While doing his duty on one side of the bush, he spied another guest doing the same on the other side: the former King of England.

JOHN COOPER FITCH

As two veterans of relatively the same age, Jack and John became friends. They exchanged their war experiences. Jack was recuperating in Florida from injuries to his back sustained when his PT Boat was sunk. John had been injured when he bailed out.

John F. Kennedy in 1945.

John recalled one particular conversation. Lying around the pool, the two wondered what they would do with the rest of their lives. John remembered remarking that Jack would never have to worry about making a living. He suggested that Jack, without the need for money, could make a significant contribution in the nation's political life. "Why don't you go to Boston where your grandfather was the mayor and get involved?" Whether or not this conversation had anything to do with the events that followed is pure conjecture. Kathleen was killed in a plane crash in 1948 and John moved to White Plains, New York.

STARTING TO RACE

After settling in New York, Fitch bought his first sports car, an MGTC. He was so enthralled with the car that he rented a few square feet in a sporting-goods store and set himself up as an MG dealer. He figured that everyone would be so enthusiastic about MGs that they would fly out of his dealership. With a sales price of $2,395 (about $25,000 in today's money) that didn't prove to be the case. He was only able to sell three that first year.

John, on the right, in front of his White Plains dealership.

JOHN COOPER FITCH

Meanwhile, the Sports Car Club of America and the MG Car Club organized an open-road race at Bridgehampton on Long Island. "The Bridge," as it is affectionately called, is located near Sag Harbor on Long Island about 100 miles from New York City. Originally, races were held on public roads in the area, which, before WWII, was lightly populated mostly with farms. The first event was held in 1915 and racing continued, off and on, until 1953 when, as the area continued to develop, it was decided not to have racing on the public road.

The course ran through Main Street in the center of town, then past farms, houses and over a bridge. That first event after WWII was held on June 11, 1949. Having sold all the MGs in his stock, Fitch borrowed a TC from one of his customers and entered. John started near the end of the pack, but, as he grew accustomed to the road, he started moving up, passing car after car. When the flag fell, he was fifth overall.

Before the race, John had assembled a small crew to help him. Among them was a woman—Elizabeth Huntley—whom he had met at a barn dance the previous year. Since then, they had been dating. Soon, he proposed marriage, which she accepted. Below: The party after the wedding.

Soon thereafter, they married and set off in a new TC for a honeymoon, driving through New England. On their way back, John proposed a detour to Linden Field, an airport in New Jersey where a road race was scheduled. Along the way, it started to rain, but they kept on with the top down. John wanted to see if he could do better than he had the previous month at The Bridge. They arrived at the last moment and John didn't have time to practice.

John and Elizabeth with the MGTC at Linden Field in New Jersey.

As the cars were lining up on the grid, he put Elizabeth on a hay bale, dumped their luggage and sped out to join the pack at the rear end. He put his cap on backwards (no helmets in those days) and took off on the 50-lap event over the five-turn 1.8-mile course. He began passing car after car and, after a time, Elizabeth's pit signals told John he was ahead. By the tenth lap, he had built up a quarter-mile lead. But only five laps from the checker, his engine overheated and he finished fourth overall and third in class.

John's last race in his first year of racing was the 1949 Watkins Glen Grand Prix held on September 17. Post WWII U.S.

JOHN COOPER FITCH

road racing had begun at the Glen the previous year. The course was 6.6 miles long using paved, gravel and dirt roads. The 1949 GP was won by Miles Collier in his Ford-Riley who finished just in front of Briggs Cunningham in a 166 Ferrari. John was fifth overall in his TC ahead of all the other MGs.

Elizabeth and John moved into a walk-up apartment in Greenwich Village and he expanded his auto agency in White Plains to include Jeeps. He called it the Sports and Utility Motors. The business included sales of new and used cars as well as a repair facility.

John's first race in 1950 was on January 3 at Palm Beach Shores, Florida. The race was won by Tom Cole's HRG. Tom and John were later to become close friends. Fitch managed to win his class in the TC.

John won his class in his MG at Palm Beach Shores in January 1950.

After that race, John decided to build his own sports car. John told me that "I decided I wanted something a bit faster than an MG, so I started a shop within my agency." Like others were later to do, he stuffed an American V-8 engine into a light and good-handling small car. He started with a Fiat 1100cc chassis housed in modified body parts from a Crosley. The engine he chose was a flathead Ford V8-60, the smallest and lightest of its genre. These engines were then being used in American Midget race cars, so tried-and-true racing parts and modifications were readily available. John dubbed the special the "Fitch Model B," but it soon acquired the moniker, "Fitch Bitch."

The first event for the "Bitch" (above) was on May 2, 1950 at an SCCA race at the Suffolk County Airport on Long Island. He had finished putting the car together just before the race, so, even though he didn't have any time for practice, John managed a second in class. After two more races, Fitch sold his "Bitch" to our mutual friend, Paul O'Shea.

JOHN COOPER FITCH

In the fall of 1950, John and Elizabeth moved from their Greenwich apartment to a two-story Dutch Colonial house in Stamford, Connecticut. With some brief sojourns, they would live in Connecticut for the rest of their lives.

At this point, I want to interject a comment. John competed in a large number of races in different cars. To write a litany of all of them would, I think, make rather dull reading. So I'm going to recount John's experiences in those that were of particular significance and/or those that make a good story.

THE FIRST SEBRING

On November 10, 1950, it was announced that a sports-car race would take place at the Sebring Air Terminal in Florida. It was the first ever held at that venue. The event was to be a six-hour race, the longest held in the U.S. for many years. It was significant in that it was the first of the annual events that take place at Sebring. Later, it became part of the so-called "Triple Crown of Road Racing" and part of the World Manufacturers' Championship.

Alec Ulmann was the promoter, as he would be for years thereafter. Alec tried to get an FIA sanction, but was unsuccessful. The race was a big deal for the city as well as the State. Governor Fuller Warren was there along with Arthur Godfrey. Women's aerobatic champion Betty Skelton performed in her midget plane before the start. The entry fee for adults was $1 and for children, 25 cents. The race, held on December 31, 1950, started at 3 p.m. and ended at 9 p.m. It was the first day-and-night race ever held in the U.S. More than 8,000 spectators turned out to watch.

Fitch's friend, Colby Whitmore, a well-known commercial illustrator at the time, persuaded John to co-drive in Colby's stock XK120 Jaguar. John and Elizabeth drove from their new home in Stamford, Connecticut to Florida in the Jaguar. Colby had John take the first turn. It was a Le Mans start with the drivers running across the track to their cars which were lined up in the order of qualifying times. Twenty-eight started and 17 managed to go the distance. John was second after the start following Phil Walters in a Cadillac-Healey. Fitch and Whitmore won their class, but the motorsports world was set on its ear when an American car, a Crosley Hotshot, won the Index of Performance with Fred Koster and Bob Deshon at the wheel. Fred Wacker in a Cadillac Allard won overall followed by Jim Kimberly in a Cadillac-Healey. Two-time Le Mans winner, Luigi Chenetti, who had moved to New York City and opened an imported-car agency, drove his 166 Ferrari without relief and finished seventh overall.

John Fitch in the XK120 Jaguar at Sebring on December 31, 1950.

Afterwards, a gala New Years Eve soirée was organized by Ulmann. John remembered that everyone had a wonderful time. During the party, Ulmann announced that a second race would take place and that it would be a 12-hour affair. It took place on March 15, 1952, this time with an FIA sanction. John talked with Briggs Cunningham at the party. Somehow the discussion got around to Fitch becoming involved with the Cunningham effort.

THE FITCH-WHITMORE SPECIAL

John and Colby's success at the first Sebring whetted their appetites. They wanted a car that would be able to compete for an overall victory, not just a class win. In addition, they enjoyed the camaraderie and teamwork involved in co-driving in a long-distance event. They even talked about entering the best-known and most famous long-distance contest of all: The 24-Hours of Le Mans.

John liked the reliability of the Jaguar running gear, but he knew that a stock XK120 was way too heavy. The two decided to build a special with a Jaguar as a basis, so they started out by buying a new XK. Next, they designed a new lightweight body and frame. Below: Fitch racing the Fitch-Whitmore Special.

Using drawings and plans made by Fitch and Whitmore, Andy Salida did the actual construction in Fitch's Sports & Utility Motors Shop. He hand-formed a frame.

With running gear installed, the car weighed in at 2,100 pounds. Stock XK120 roadsters weighed 2,921 pounds. Fitch installed front torsion bars, semi-ellipticals in the rear and Alfin drum brakes. In addition, he lowered the rear end and fitted hotter cams in the Jaguar engine which otherwise remained stock. Sixteen-inch Borrani wire wheels replaced the stock steel rims. The Fitch-Whitmore was, and still is, uncommonly beautiful.

With its intended use in mind, the partners called it the "Le Mans Special." But they soon came to the conclusion that, with exposed wheels and cycle fenders, the car wouldn't be able to attain the necessary top speed to be competitive due to the long straights at Le Mans. It turned out to be much more suited to the shorter U.S. circuits of the time. It had excellent acceleration, braking and handling.

The first race for their special was the May 26, 1951 Bridgehampton (above) where John won his class and came in fourth overall. Also, that day, Fitch folded his lanky frame into a 500cc Effy-Jap and won the very first Formula III event held in the U.S.

Fitch, as well as Whitmore, raced it a few more times that year. By then John was fully on board with the Cunningham team, so they sold the special to Gerry Georgi of Nyack, New York. Gerry installed a Buick V-8 engine and raced it for a few years. Georgi sold it to Jim Haynes in 1974, who removed the Buick, installed a Jag engine and raced it for the next 24 years. When Jim decided to part with it, he had Joel Finn sell it in 1987. Afterwards, the car was restored to its original condition and vintage raced by a number of owners. After changing hands a few more times, in 2011, it was auctioned off at Amelia Island for $198,000.

The Fitch-Whitmore, although perhaps the best-known, wasn't John's only foray into car creation. The first of his cars to hit the track, of course, was the "Fitch Bitch."

FIRST INTERNATIONAL RACE

In 1943, a military junta led by Colonel Juan Perón (right, with Evita) took over the government of Argentina. Perón, a motor-racing enthusiast, was elected president in 1946. He wanted to stage a Formula One event in Buenos Aires, but the FIA requires a preliminary event to take place on the circuit in order to test it out. So he organized a sports-car race that took place on February 18, 1951. Perón had Argentine boxer

Luis Firpo helping him. Firpo asked Alec Ulmann to organize a group of American cars and drivers to supplement the Argentine entrants. Ulmann recruited George Rand, Jim Kimberly, Bill Spear, Fred Wacker, Tom Cole and Bruce Stevenson among others. But Stevenson couldn't take the time off from his job, so he recommended John Fitch. Perón offered to pay their way plus expenses for themselves as well as their cars. John wanted to go, but he didn't have a car he felt would be competitive.

Tom Cole had damaged his Allard in an accident at Watkins Glen, so he acquired a new one, fitted with a new Chrysler Hemi engine, for Argentina. John asked Tom if he could enter the old Allard if he could repair it in time and Tom agreed. Elizabeth was not exactly ecstatic about John's idea to travel to Argentina. She was six months pregnant with their first child and decided to remain at home. John called the event, "My greatest racing opportunity to date."

John got to work. One problem was that the frame had been dented on one side. John remembered that "I chained the right front of the car to a tree and backed up gingerly. There was a shock as the chain reached its limit, and, after each incremental shock, I measured one side of the frame against the other side, which had not been pushed in. When it came back to the right place, I stopped." He was barely able to finish on time and load the old Allard aboard the ship, the S.S. Rio Jachal. Fitch stuffed a bunch of spare parts along with his clothes in bags and took a flight for Buenos Aires in an Argentine State Airlines DC-6.

When he arrived, John spent a full week there getting the Allard ready. Although Perón offered as many mechanics as needed without charge, John couldn't speak any Spanish. So he went ahead and did all the work himself. Taking sufficient time was difficult. Every evening there was some sort of a party and, during the day, the Americans were expected to attend various functions.

As race day approached, John worked feverishly, making air scoops and drilling the backing plates to cool the brakes. He replaced the carburetors and manifold with a spare set he had brought. The main competition was Cole in his new Allard, Fred Wacker in another Allard plus Jim Kimberly and Bill Spear in Ferraris. In addition, there was Argentine Adolfo Schwelm Cruz, who had won his class at the 1950 Mille Miglia and Targa Florio driving a 2.5 SS Alfa Superleggera.

The 2.2-mile course was on the city streets and very bumpy, and, in some places, really rough. In practice, Fitch was able to do the third fastest behind Wacker and Cruz. All around the course an enormous crowd was on hand on race day. All the entrants lined up for the Le Mans start in front of a box holding Perón, his wife,

Evita, and other dignitaries. John was second away, but at the end of the first lap had pulled ahead closely followed by Cole, Cruz and Wacker. Tom kept trying to pass, but on the eighth lap, his gearbox failed and he had to drop out. A few laps after that, Cruz pulled out with a smoking engine. This left John with a clear lead, but soon Wacker, caught up and John had to strain to hold the lead. When Fred tried to pass on a U-turn, he went off the course and got back on the course a lap behind John. Just before Wacker spun out, John set the fastest lap of the day—and ever for that circuit—at 2:13.5

John Fitch in the Allard at Buenos Aires.

Fitch took the checker and won his first victory in an international event. As all race fans know, a winner is kissed by the race queen and presented with the trophy. In this case, the race queen was also the queen of the country, one Evita Perón. The next day, John and the other drivers were invited to a party hosted by Perón and Fitch was formally introduced to Evita.

JOHN COOPER FITCH

She spoke to him in rapid Spanish and presented him with a lapel pin that signified he was an honorary member of the Perónista Party. Although she was vivacious and clearly a political asset for her husband, John noticed she didn't seem all that well. Actually, she was afflicted with cancer and died the following year.

Evita Perón

1951 LE MANS

In 1951, Briggs Cunningham called John and invited him to be a part of the Cunningham team at the 24-Hours of Le Mans that June. Briggs Swift Cunningham (1907-2003) came from a wealthy family. His grandfather had founded the Proctor & Gamble Co. Consequently, he never had to work a day in his life. He did virtually everything there was to do in the world of motorsports. He constructed and drove sports-racing cars as well as ran his own team. In addition he manufactured sports cars, had an auto museum open to the public and maintained a very large library of books about cars and boats. Almost as well-known in the world of yachting as in motor-racing, he won the Americas' Cup in 1958.

Cunningham drove one of his early creations, his Bu-Merc at the first U.S. post-war event at Watkins Glen in 1948. The car had a pre-war Buick Century engine on a 1936 Buick chassis with bits and pieces put together from a Mercedes-Benz body. Briggs was second in a preliminary 4-lap qualifier and third in the main event.

Cunningham had given Le Mans a try in 1950. His dream was to win with an American-built car with American drivers. That year, he entered two Cadillacs. One was stock and the other, a Cadillac-engined special—dubbed by the French "Le Monstré"—fitted with an extremely ugly body. With Miles and Sam Collier in the stock car plus Phil Walters and Briggs himself in "Le Monstré," they surprised the motorsports world. The stock Caddy finished 10th overall with "Le Monstré" just behind in 11th.

JOHN COOPER FITCH

Phil Walters in the Cadillac and Briggs Cunningham in his "Le Monstré" at the 24-Hours of Le Mans in 1950.

In order to achieve his goal, Cunningham knew he had to come up with better machinery. So he and his team went home to West Palm Beach, Florida. Briggs decided the answer was to design and make his own cars. The first—the Cunningham C-1—was finished in late 1950. Although initially more were planned, as it turned out, only one example was made. A C-2 followed in 1951. The C-2 had a Chrysler Hemi engine rather than the Cadillac that was in the C-1. Three were made as sports-racing cars and designated C-2R. They were finished by May 1951 and shipped to France for that year's Le Mans.

Fitch sailed to France along with the rest of the team and cars. Just before they left, John and Elizabeth's first child, John Huntley Fitch, was born on June 7. John was reluctant to leave so soon, but Elizabeth agreed he should go as such an opportunity might never again arise.

The works C-Type Jaguar of Peter Walker/Peter Whitehead leads the Cunning-ham/Huntoon C2-R and the Fitch/Walters C2-R at the 1951 Le Mans.

Cunningham assigned Fitch and Phil Walters to drive C-2R #4, George Rand and Fred Wacker in #5 and himself with George Huntoon in #3. Fitch and Walters were, arguably, the best drivers among the six. The main challenge for the team was the new Jaguar C-Types. A young Stirling Moss set the fastest time in a C; Peter Walker and Peter Whitehead in another C ended up winning. The Rand/Wacker C-4R dropped out after 76 laps; the Cunning-ham/Huntoon car after 98 laps, both with various mechanical problems. But, to the amazement of most aficionados, the Fitch/Walter car was running second overall at the 18th hour behind the Walker/Whitehead C-Type Jaguar. Then the Chrysler Hemi in the Rand/Wacker C-2R burned its bearings and valves, consequently slowed, but nevertheless managed to finish in 18th. The Fitch/Walters C-2R finished in third. "Had we managed to win,"

Fitch remarked, "it would have been the biggest upset in Le Mans history."

In August 1951, Briggs took the team to Elkhart Lake. Twenty-six cars ran the main event, the Elkhart Lake Cup. John Fitch and John Gordon Bennett in a Cunningham-entered Cad-Allard were on the front row. John held the lead for five laps when Phil Walters in a C-4R coupe passed. On the 13th, Fitch took the lead again while Briggs in the second C-4R moved up to third. Phil Hill in a C-Type Jaguar passed Cunningham, but had to fall back when exhaust got into the cockpit. At the finish, Fitch won with Walters and Cunningham following, a clean-sweep for the Cunningham team.

The next month, the team went to Watkins Glen. Phil Walters won the 15-lap main event followed by Fitch, both in Cunninghams. In a preliminary race—the Seneca Cup—John drove Briggs' Ferrari coupé to second. By the end of that year's season, John Fitch would be crowned the first SCCA National Champion. From then on, Fitch became an integral part of the Cunningham team. John and Briggs also became life-long friends.

The Walters/Cunningham followed by the Fitch Cunningham at the start of the September 1951 main event at Watkins Glen, NY.

1951 MEXICO

For John, competition during 1951 wasn't quite over. His friend, Carl Kiekhaefer, asked him to drive a 1951 Chrysler Saratoga stock car in the Carrera Panamericana, the Mexican Road Race. It's interesting to note that when Kiekhaefer entered Chryslers, they had "Mercury" on them. This could be confusing since Chrysler also made cars called Mercurys. The reason was that Kiekhaefer owned the Mercury Outboard Motor Company and Mercury was the brand-name of the Kiekhaefer Corporation.

The Mexican race is considered by many to be the most challenging and dangerous ever run. The first was held in 1950; the last in 1954. The route is the entire length of Mexico from the U.S. border to that with Guatemala, some 2,000 miles to the south. The reason behind the event was that a road—The Pan-American Highway—was under construction from Alaska to the bottom of South America. The Mexican leg was the first to be completed.

The 1951 race started at Tuxla Gutiérrez in the south to Ciudad Juárez in the north. It was run in six legs, beginning on November 20 and ending on November 25. Cars were flagged off each day at one minute intervals.

This was John's first time racing an American stock car. He started after 31 entries had left before him. The first leg ended at Oaxaca. From the start, Fitch passed car after car. Kiekhaefer, in a private plane, was following John from the air. Eventually Fitch passed every other car in the stock-class except Troy Ruttman in a Ford. From the air, Carl Kickhaefer could see that John was gaining on Troy when, after 320 miles and just one mile short of Oaxaca, the Chrysler engine quit. The radiator had been leaking. When

a small Mexican boy came along selling bottles of soda water,
John bought them and poured the water into the steaming radiator.
Then he tried to re-start the engine, but finally the battery failed.
Since they were only a mile from the end of the leg, John and his
navigator, Don Williams, got out and started pushing it towards the
line. But the car was very heavy, so finally, they collapsed in
exhaustion.

A 1951 Chrysler Saratoga leading a Cadillac in Mexico.

During the race, two drivers were killed. Mexican driver
José Estrada and his navigator Miguel Gonzáles died when their
Packard went off the road and over a cliff. Carlos Panini went into
a solid rock wall. Afterwards, Fitch was to recall, "Everything was
extremely difficult: the vast country, the lack of supplies, the endless road; even gasoline and food were not easily found where you
may need them." As it turned out, John's first Mexican odyssey led
to notable adventures to come.

1951 SCCA NATIONAL CHAMPION

Even then, John's 1951 racing season wasn't quite over. The event at Palm Beach, Florida, was the last SCCA National of the year. Held on December 8, Fitch was entered in two different races. The first one, which lasted for one hour—The Hoffman Trophy—was for "unmodified" (i.e. production) Jaguars. After a spirited battle with Karl Brocken, John won.

His next race—the main event—followed immediately thereafter. It was called the "Riviera Cup" and lasted for two hours. John drove a 340 America Ferrari belonging to Bill Spear. Bill was also an entrant in his 166 Mille Miglia Ferrari. Briggs Cunningham was in a similar Ferrari. Briggs had entered Phil Walters in a Healey Silverstone with a six-liter Cadillac engine. Tom Cole was in the Chrysler-Allard that he drove in Argentina and Fred Wacker in a Cadillac-Allard. Paul O'Shea entered the Fitch Model B (the Fitch Bitch) that he had bought from John.

When the race started, Tom Cole forged in front, but was hit by another car. The Allard's gas tank was partially crushed and caught fire. Cole continued on without noticing the flames. When the front runners got to the main straight, Tom saw that his car was on fire and stopped to put it out. Walters in the Healey took the lead and kept it for 15 laps when John came up on Phil's tail. After a number of intense laps, Phil had to pull into the pits when the Cadillac engine failed. This left Fitch in front by a wide margin and he took the checkered flag. Wacker was second in the Allard with Cunningham in his Ferrari third. The best Paul O'Shea could do was eighth overall and third in Class 4.

The SCCA established its National Sports Car Championship in 1951 and John Fitch was its first winner. He had won in Buenos Aires, at Elkhart Lake and Allentown and Palm Beach. In addition he scored eight wins and was second overall four times. That year started Fitch off on a career as a professional race driver as well as one that was being noticed in the press.

John's career was to expand exponentially, however, in 1952. The Cunningham team was off to France again. They left New York on the S.S. Mauretania; this time Elizabeth came along with young John in tow. Briggs had entered Fitch and George Rice in a C-4R. On the very first lap with John up, a coil lead in the engine popped out and he had to make a pit stop. After a quick fix, he rejoined the race in dead-last. Determined to catch up, Fitch set a new official Le Mans lap record. By the fourth hour, the Fitch/Rice C-4R was in third place when the engine failed completely.

The 1951 Le Mans Cunningham team, John Fitch in the middle.

THE NÜRBURGRING

The 1952 Le Mans, however, provided John with future possibilities. He met Daimler Benz engineer Rudolf Uhlenhaut. A new Mercedes Benz 300 SL came in first and second that year at Le Mans. At that point, John knew that the era of the Cunningham C cars would come to an end. Wanting to further his career, John looked up Rudy and congratulated him on the win. Uhlenhaut had taken note of how well John was doing in the Cunningham. So Rudy asked John if he would like to give a 300 SL a try. They arranged for Fitch to come to the German Grand Prix at the Nürburgring that would be held on August 3. He was to take his "drive" in the SL the day after the race.

In the meanwhile, Ferry Porsche, taking notice of John's Le Mans lap record drive, invited him to compete in an all-Porsche race that would take place at the 'Ring on August 1. On arrival, John found Porsche Team Manager Huschke von Hanstein in the Porsche paddock. John was assigned to drive a 356 Coupé. After six practice laps on one of the World's most demanding and difficult race courses—the 14-mile circuit has 174 turns—he joined the starting grid.

The majority of the other Porsche drivers were Germans who were very experienced driving the Nürburgring. John was in the middle of 24 other Porsches on the grid. When the flag dropped, all got away closely grouped since all had similar power. At the end of the first lap, John was in fifth place. When the car ahead ran off the road, John was in fourth. With increasing familiarity with the course, John settled down to a steady drive. On the last lap, the car in third place dropped out and Fitch was able to finish in third. Both von Hanstein and Dr. Porsche were not just pleased, they were a little amazed. It was an outstanding effort for a first-timer at the 'Ring.

John in the Porsche (#67) at the Nürburgring.

In another race preliminary to the next day's Grand Prix, four 300 SLs took the first four places and broke a number of Nürburgring records. As he watched, John knew that he would soon be at the wheel of one of them and that his performance would be judged not only by Rudy Uhlenhaut, but also Mercedes Benz Team Manager Alfred Neubauer.

The day after the Grand Prix dawned sunny and clear. The Mercedes team was still on hand, testing the 300 SLs. John, Elizabeth and John Jr. were at the Sporthotel adjacent to the pits. John was nervous, but Elizabeth told him to calm down.

After lunch, Herr Neubauer told John they were ready for him. He was admonished not to let the engine speed exceed 6,000 rpm. After a warm-up lap, he pushed the SL to the point he felt he could without taking any untoward chances. At the fastest section of the track, he got up to 145 mph. Finally, it was over and John was glad to get out of the car. The mechanics looked it over to make sure there weren't any scratches or dents. One checked the tachometer tell-tale that showed the maximum rpm achieved. It sat at 5,800. Neubauer seemed pleased with John's performance. Thinking that lap might have been a fluke, he asked John to take another lap during which he managed to shave a few seconds off his previous effort.

Alfred Neubauer, John Fitch and Rudy Uhlenhaut.

Afterwards, John talked to Neubauer and Uhlenhaut about that year's Mexican Road Race. He pointed out that he thought the 300 SLs were ideal for the most demanding of races and that a good showing there would enhance sales in the U.S. Neubauer said he might be interested, but that the time and money available had to be considered.

1952 WITH THE CUNNINGHAM TEAM

The Fitch family returned to the U.S. and John joined the Cunningham équipe for an August 17, 1952 SCCA race on the new course at Thompson, Connecticut. Phil Walters and Fitch were in C-4Rs, John in a roadster, Phil in a new coupé. Phil won with John second.

After John came home, he received a letter from Neubauer asking a number of questions about the Mexican race. Consequently, they engaged in a rather lengthy correspondence in which Fitch wrote about the race at great length with details about such things as rainfall and temperature. John emphasized the importance of the right tires and hinted that he would be available should Daimler Benz decide to enter. He more or less convinced Neubauer to give Mexico a try.

The next month the Cunningham team went to Elkhart Lake where John had won the 200-mile main the previous year. The event had become popular and, in spite of its rather remote location, attracted a reported 100,000 spectators for the 1952 race. Phil Hill defeated Phil Walters and won one of the preliminary contests—the Sheldon Cup—in Hollywood Jaguar dealer Charles Hornburg's C-Type. Briggs entered C-4Rs for Fitch, Walters and himself in the 31-lap main event. Irving Robbins, not part of the team, entered a C-2R. These three dominated, finishing one, two, and three. John won again and, in doing so, established a new record of 2 hours, 16:13.4 minutes, averaging 87.5 mph. Hill managed a fourth in the C-Type. As it turned out, this was the last race on the roads around Elkhart Lake. A purpose-built course—Road America—was completed in 1955 only a few miles away.

Fitting two events into a single month, the Cunningham effort went to Watkins Glen for the 5th Annual Grand Prix held on September 19-20. A huge audience, estimated at more than 250,000, crowded around the public-road course making practice difficult. Passing on the right and in corners was not allowed.

John in the C-Type Jaguar at Watkins Glen in 1952.

In his first factory ride, John Fitch drove a new C-Type to victory in the 53-mile preliminary Seneca Cup with Jaguar President Sir William Lyons looking on. Then, Phil Walters and Briggs Cunningham lined up in C-4Rs for the main event. Fred Wacker in an Allard was on the pole with Briggs beside him. At the end of the first lap, they crossed Start/Finish side by side. Just afterwards, the Allard slid to the side of the course and hit 12 spectators including a seven-year-old boy who was killed. The race was black-flagged and the injured were taken to the hospital. Although officials tried to re-start the race, they were not able to because onlookers had crowded onto the track in several places. So the event was cancelled. This was the second such tragedy at the Glen. In 1950, Sam Collier, a fireman and two spectators lost their lives when Collier rolled his car and left the road. This wasn't the first time Fitch would witness disaster on a track, nor, unfortunately, would it be the last.

General Curtis LeMay, head of the Strategic Air Command and a sports-car aficionado, after noting injuries and deaths on open-road races, decided the safest venues would be Air Force Base runways. The first was held on October 26 at Turner Air Force Base near Albany, Georgia. Serendipitously, this base was where John Fitch had taken his advance flight training in 1941. General LeMay, with his wife riding shotgun, drove his Allard all the way from Omaha, Nebraska. On arrival, he entered the Allard for Roy Scott to drive in a preliminary race where Scott finished third. The Air Force MPs and other airmen, along with SCCA officials, were able to bring off what some considered the safest road race to date.

Briggs entered his usual drivers: Fitch, Walters and himself in C-4Rs. Some 60,000 spectators, none of whom were allowed anywhere near the course, saw John, Bill Spear and Marshall Lewis in Ferraris duel for the lead during much of the four hours. Towards the end, Fitch was able to take the lead and won 12.3 seconds ahead of Lewis. To top it off, General LeMay personally awarded the trophy to John.

When he returned home from Georgia, a telegram from Neubauer had arrived asking Fitch if he was available to drive in the Panamericana. If so, he was instructed to leave immediately for Mexico City. Naturally, John sent a telegram back that he would be there. Like his war years and his sojourns to Argentina and Le Mans, Fitch was about to set off on another life-changing adventure.

THE 1952 MEXICAN ROAD RACE

The Carrera Panamericana that year was scheduled to leave Tuxla Gutiérrez on November 19, 1952. John arrived at the capitol on October 28 with not a whole lot of time to prepare for taking part in a major international race with a world-class team.

During his Mexican drive the previous year, he had only experienced the road from Tuxla Gutiérrez to Oaxaca, just 321 miles out of a total 2,135. He was yet to appreciate the difficulty, danger and challenge of the totality.

During the seventies, I drove much of it during a number of excursions. The changes of climate and conditions in Mexico during November are extreme. The race starts in the steaming tropics and traverses deserts and mountain ranges of more than 10,000 feet where it often snows. The road twists back and forth like the tightest of Alpine passes, and then often runs straight as an arrow for many miles. Road conditions and surfaces then varied from flat and smooth to rough and steep. Accidents and fatalities were (and still are) common. To top it off, and even though the Mexican government tried to close the roads during the races, it wasn't uncommon to encounter wandering domestic, as well as wild, animals and an occasional pedestrian.

Neubauer assigned Herman Lang, Karl Kling and John Fitch to drive. Accompanying them were navigators Erwin Grupp, Hans Klenk and Eugen Geiger. Daimler Benz brought three 300 SL cars to race, an additional car for practicing, two passenger cars, two 3½-ton trucks, a large quantity of spare parts and 35 people. The top of the Fitch car had been removed, making it into a roadster. All this was supplemented by the Mexican Mercedes Benz distributor.

The 1952 Mercedes Benz Mexico team; Fitch and Geiger on the far right.

Also competing were some of the World's best sports cars. Included were Ferrari and Lancia from Italy, Gordini from France, Jaguar from England as well as Mercedes and Porsche from Germany. Joining a number of Mexican drivers were World Champion Alberto Ascari, Luigi Villoresi, Robert Manzon, Jean Behra and Umberto Maglioli to name a few. John's and my lifelong friends, Phil Hill and Jack McAfee were in Ferraris; Jack in Ernie McAfee's (no relation). Plus, as usual, there were a number of American stock car drivers, among them Bill Stroppe, Chuck Stevenson, Johnny Manz and Walt Faulkner. There were two classes, one for sports and touring cars, the other for stockers.

Eighty-seven competitors lined up single-file at Tuxla Gutiérrez, in the order that entries were received. Crowds lined both sides of the road, even spilling over onto it. At 6:30 a.m., the Starter waved off the first car, a Cadillac driven by the son of Mexican President Alemán. Next off one minute later was a Jaguar, then

JOHN COOPER FITCH

Herman Lang (300 SL), Karl Kling (300 SL), a Ferrari and then John Fitch.

John remembered that he had to start slowly. Due to the dense crowd of spectators, it was hard to see ahead. After a few minutes, however, and with a clear road ahead, he put pedal to the metal. Soon he passed the Ferrari that had started a minute before him and then the Cadillac that had started first. The Fitch 300 SL roadster had lower gearing, but, since it was lighter, was faster than the coupes.

Fitch and Geiger lining up just before the start.

Fitch and his navigator, Eugen Geiger, had agreed on a number of different hand signals, as neither of them spoke the other's language. As they approached a single-lane bridge made from boards nailed to cross ties, Eugen signaled John to slow down.

Then they descended from a mountain to a valley where the turns were shrouded by clouds. They approached village after village where they had to slow due to the onlookers. Finally in the clear, John and Eugen were able to pass not only Lang, but also Kling. Fitch realized that perhaps they were then in the lead. Going through a dip at 140 mph, the car became momentarily airborne and started to violently shake. When John was able to stop, they got out and saw that one of the rear tires was all but gone and the wheel was severely bent. As they were changing the wheel, Kling re-passed.

When they got back on the road, it became obvious that all wasn't well. The car wandered on the straights and hopped when cornering. They stopped again to take a look, but decided there was nothing to do about it on the road. So they continued at much reduced speeds to their tire stop, 170 miles from Tuxla Gutiérrez. After changing both rear tires and replacing both spares, they got back on the road.

The suspension problem, however, hadn't gone away. And the clutch started to slip. Finally, they arrived at Oaxaca, passed the checker and drove to the garage Mercedes had rented. After Neubauer greeted them, they explained the problems. The mechanics went to work and discovered the suspension problem was a broken shock. Kling in another 300 SL had a problem too. A huge buzzard broke the windshield. Kling was slightly injured, but his navigator, Klenk, was knocked out. Afterwards, "Buzzard Bars" were installed in front of the windshield.

Everyone lined up again the next morning at 6:30 a.m. to set off on two legs to Mexico City. The first was Puebla, 250 miles away over a mountain road. After Puebla, it was 81 miles over a 9,800 foot pass to Mexico City.

Fitch remembered this part clearly. In his own words: "The road was truly treacherous, climbing and descending at severe angles, sometimes wheeling and reversing like a monstrous roller coaster, flanked by gaping crevices and sheer cliff overhanging rock-strewn river beds, often a thousand feet below." During the previous year, three drivers had lost their lives in this section.

The Fitch/Geiger 300 SL had been repaired and was running well. They passed Chinetti, Maglioli and McAfee over a fast section before the mountains. In some places, the crowds pressed too close to the road and some would dash right in front of the speeding car. While going some 130 mph, they noticed black tire tracks running straight off the road towards a steep drop off. When they got to Puebla, they learned it was Jean Behra, who was injured. In addition, a Mexican driver in an XK120 Jaguar was killed when he hit a bridge. At Puebla, Fitch and Geiger learned they were running fourth overall.   Below: John driving the Mercedes Benz.

After Puebla came the highest part of the mountain range. As John negotiated the narrow road, Villoresi in his Ferrari got closer and closer until finally they were nose to tail. Realizing the Ferrari had a more powerful engine, Fitch pulled over and waved Luigi by. As they approached Mexico City, crowds lined the road, kept in check by police. Just before the finish, a large dog trotted in front of the 300 SL. John swerved and narrowly missed it.

Mexico City marked the completion of one-third of the race. They had covered 661 miles with another 1,273 to go. They had arrived on November 20, the day Mexicans mark the start of their revolution to free the country from Spain. It is their Fourth of July. The arrival of the participants in the Carrera had been timed to coincide with the celebration.

The next day, Fitch and his 300 SL left Mexico City for the next leg, 267 miles to Leon. He was in third behind Bracco and Kling. After 50 miles on the road, one of his tires threw a tread. So they were back to changing one of the two spares. John set out again, but by now cautious due to the tires, he didn't exceed 130 mph, much slower than the others. At Leon, they had only a half an hour to refuel and change tires. The next leg was 330 miles north to Durango.

Then things started to go their way, passing both Lang and Kling. But when Fitch put the pedal to the metal, the car slowed and Kling re-passed. After this repeated three times, John fell back and followed Kling. The leading 300 SL kept throwing up gravel and sand, hitting John in the face. But he was prepared. Ever the inventor, he had devised a leather mask to fit under his goggles. On the next straight, the car started to shimmy as though the front wheels were out of alignment. They stopped to take a look and found one of the front tires badly worn. So they changed, using the second spare. When they went over 100 mph, however, the shimmying started again. After what seemed like an endless time at slow speeds, they arrived at Durango.

When the Mercedes engineer and mechanics examined the Fitch car, it was discovered that a loose spring hanger threw off the alignment. The hanger was replaced and larger air scoops (devised by Fitch), were installed to cool the brakes. A major problem arose because the tire balancing machinery had been damaged at Mexico City.

JOHN COOPER FITCH

The next leg was to Parral, 251 miles to the north. Soon after leaving Durango, the shimmying started again, preventing them from going faster than about 120 mph. After the long run, Fitch and Geiger pulled into a gas station. There were only two stalls, both occupied by Kling and Lang. Finally they pulled out and work on the Fitch 300 SL could start. Geiger tried to adjust the alignment, but the equipment was in Mexico City. So Fitch held up a stick while Geiger made adjustments. When they drove to the starting line, it appeared the steering was even worse. They had to return to the gas station where a mechanic reset the tie rod. When they left Parral, the tires howled in protest and it was apparent they couldn't continue. Returning again to the gas station, the alignment was reset again.

Back at the starting line for the second time, they set off, but after 20 miles and at about 145 mph, the left rear tire blew. After changing it, they continued with Fitch keeping his speed at a steady 135 mph. They crossed the line at Chihuahua, having lost about 15 minutes on the leg. The pair had to appear before the race committee there where they were told that any repairs had to be made at the side of the road. The rule had been violated when, after starting from Parral, they returned to the gas station. At Chihuahua, they were fourth overall.

The last day's run was to Juarez where the weather report said it was snowing. About 50 miles from the city, they ran into a strong cross wind that shifted the car all across the road. As they approached the finish line, many small planes were above, flying along with them. About 30 miles from the end, Fitch and Geiger passed Lang.

As they got to the city, crowds of spectators were thicker and thicker. When the checkered flag waved, the Fitch/Geiger 300 SL was fourth overall. Karl Kling won with a total elapsed time of 18 hours, 51 minutes and 19 seconds. Lang was second and Luigi Chinetti third in a Ferrari Mexico. The fourth place, however, was not recognized because they were disqualified due to returning to the gas station at Parral. In consolation, Fitch had recorded the highest average speed of 135 mph—a one-stage record—on the final 230 mile leg from Chihuahua to Juarez. It was so fast that the airplanes following the race were unable to keep up. Out of 84 cars that started, only 39 survived to finish. The fact that Neubauer was happy with Fitch's performance was a harbinger of things to come.

John didn't race again for the rest of 1952. Elizabeth was happy that he would spend some quality time at home.

The Mercedes Benz team celebrating their 1952 Mexico win.

THE MONTE CARLO RALLY

Rallying is a quite different sport than racing. It's widely popular with amateur as well as professional events taking place all over the world. There may be more actual participants who rally than race. The idea of a rally is to drive a set route in a certain amount of time. Each car has a driver and a navigator, whose task it is to make sure they stay on the route and drive it in the set amount of time. To put it another way, a rally is a race against time. Rallies usually consist of a number of legs. The winner is the car that accumulates the least time lost.

Perhaps the most famous of all is the Monte Carlo. It started in 1911 and, except for the two world-war years, continues to this day. It takes place during the dead of winter with competitors battling ice, cold and snow. The Monte Carlo is difficult, even for Grand Prix drivers who sometimes compete. It also includes hill climbs as well as timed and regularity runs.

Over the years, routes have changed, but in 1953 there were seven starting points: Glasgow, Lisbon, Munich, Oslo, Palermo, Stockholm and Monte Carlo itself. Its 2,000 miles traversed the entire continent of Europe. The event that year was for sedans. It started on January 20 and ended four days later in Monte Carlo.

Fitch was employed by Rootes Motors to co-drive a Sunbeam-Talbot. The team included driver Peter Collins and navigator John Cutts. Since the contest was non-stop, one driver drove while the other slept in the back seat. After lunching at the Royal Scottish Automobile Club, the team started out from Glasgow. When they arrived at Dover, they took the ferry across the channel to France and then on to Paris. Then, regardless of the starting city, all entrants converged on Bourges. From there, the route over the Alps was the same for everyone.   Below: traversing the Alps.

After traversing 2,000 miles across Europe, of the total of 440 cars who started from the various cities, only 253 survived to arrive in Monte Carlo. Astonishingly, the Sunbeam-Talbot team had not accumulated any penalties.

When the competitors arrived at Monte Carlo, they were impounded in a "parc fermé," a parking lot sealed off so that repairs or alterations couldn't be made on any of the cars. The following day there was a test that involved accelerating from a dead stop 220 yards, stopping, backing up and going forward 55 yards. The Sunbeam-Talbot failed the test when the gearbox refused to go into reverse for a second or two. They were eliminated along with 153 others. The final leg of the rally was a 50-mile regularity run over the mountains around Monte Carlo. But of course the Fitch/Collins/Cutts car wasn't among the "final 100."

JOHN COOPER FITCH

Elizabeth and young John had accompanied Fitch to Europe for the rally. Afterwards, the family returned to the U.S. For much of 1953, John drove for Briggs Cunningham. The first was at MacDill Air Force Base in Tampa, Florida on February 21. The main event—a six-hour enduro—began with a Le Mans start. It was the debut of Briggs Cunningham's new C-4R. The main competition was from Phil Hill, who co-drove with Bill Spear in a 4.1 Ferrari. John Fitch in the C-4R led off, but with two hours to go, Phil passed into the lead. Suddenly, a wheel fell off the Ferrari and Hill limped into his pit on the brake drum. With the fix complete, Phil returned and started to gain on John. There wasn't enough time, however, and Hill finished in second. Briggs, driving an OSCA, won the Index of Performance.

Next on the schedule was the 12-Hours of Sebring. The previous year, the event had been the first 12-hour affair. In 1953, it increased in importance because the FIA had added it to the World Sports Car Championship. Even so, Briggs wanted to save most of his team for Le Mans; he entered just one C-4R, driven by his two top drivers: John Fitch and Phil Walters. Briggs himself entered his OSCA with Bill Lloyd co-driving.

Phil Walters (who entered U.S. pro races as "Ted Tappet" so he wouldn't lose his "amateur" status) ran across the track to the C-4R, quickly took the lead and held it for his three-hour stint. Just before Phil was about to come in for a driver change, Peter Collins in an Aston Martin DB3 passed Phil, but an XK-120 Jaguar driven by Austin Conley collided with the DB3 thus ending Collins' challenge. So when John took over the C-4R, he was in front. From then on, the Fitch/Walters Cunningham kept the lead and took the checkered flag at midnight. A factory Aston Martin DB3 was second with a C-Type Jaguar in third. Briggs, along with Mercedes Benz and Ferrari were saving their big guns for Le Mans. (The Ferraris at Sebring were not factory entries.)

THE 1953 MILLE MIGLIA

On April 25, 1953, John Fitch entered the classic long-distance race, the Mille Miglia, in Italy for the first time. In Italian, the name of the race means 1,000 miles. The distance was 1,600 kilometers, equal to 1,000 old Roman miles, or miglia. The first was held in 1927, the last in 1957. It was a yearly happening except during WWII. Some of the world's top drivers competed; Nuvolari won twice (1931 and 1933). Other winners included Caracciola, Varsi, Villoresi, Ascari, Moss and Taruffi. The route, which changed a few times, was always in northern Italy. The 1953-57 route started in Brescia, went east to Verona and Padua, south to Ferrara, southeast to Ravena, along the coastline to Pescara, then inland over the mountains to Rome. From the capital, the course went north through the Apennines to Florence, Bologna, Modena, northwest to Piacenza and back to the end at Brescia.

Through the countryside, towns, cities and mountains, road surfaces changed from smooth to very rough. Some of the roads and streets were built during Roman times. Although not as difficult as the Carrera Panamericana, the Mille Miglia, along with the Targa Florio, was challenging for both cars and drivers.

In 1957, disaster struck when the Marquis de Portago and his navigator, Edward Nelson, crashed, killing themselves as well as 11 spectators. By then, traffic in Italy had grown and it was difficult to close the roads for the race. This, as well as the accident, caused the demise of the race. In later years, regularity runs and vintage-type rallies have taken place over the course.

JOHN COOPER FITCH

Shortly after Sebring, Fitch and Donald Healey went to Detroit to meet with George Mason, president of the Nash-Kelvinator Corporation and George Romney, Mason's right-hand man. The purpose of the meeting was to plan entering a Nash-Healey in the 1953 Mille Miglia with John driving.

In 1949, Donald Healey had designed and built the Nash-Healey which had a Nash engine and transmission. The cars were made in England by Healey, then sent to the U.S. and marketed by Nash dealers. Later, rollers were shipped to Italy where re-styled bodies were installed by Pinin Farina. Production ended in 1954 after a total of 506 had been sold. The problem was that the retail price was more than that of an XK120 and the Jaguar could out-perform the Nash-Healey.

John Fitch and navigator, Ray Willday at the Mille Miglia starting line.

The concept behind the entry was to garner publicity in an effort to save the Nash-Healey image and, hopefully, spur sales. Mason and Healey were in favor of the project, but Romney was opposed. Nevertheless, they went ahead with a factory entry.

John remembered the race for me in my book, *Racing Sports Cars, Memories of the Fifties:* "In my opinion, the car was too heavy to be really competitive. My navigator, Raymond Willday, was English and a relative of Donald Healey. A day or so before the race, I tested the car and felt the brakes were poor. Then I discovered the rears weren't working at all. The tires were Dunlops and as hard as Bakelite. I persuaded Nash to violate their contract with Dunlop and install Pirellis. With brake and tire problems solved, I felt our prospects were improved."

When John arrived in Italy, he had been supplied with a Nash Ambassador sedan for him to practice with. Nino Farina, 1950 World Driving Champion, was also there to practice in a C-Type Jaguar. But it had broken its axle. So he asked Fitch if he could ride along in the Ambassador. Farina ended up driving most of the time with John taking notes. John remembered that Farina at the wheel was an "unsettling experience," weaving at high speeds through heavy traffic, bicyclists and farm carts. He was happy to arrive back in one piece.

While there, John stayed with Count Aymo Maggi in his lavish villa. There were some great parties with the likes of Peter Collins, Stirling Moss and Reg Parnell to name only a few. "Wacky" Arnolt (who conceived the Arnolt-Bristol) was there too.

Donald Healey put John Gibson in charge of the Nash-Healey effort. Just before dawn on race day, Fitch, Willday, and Gibson pushed the car slowly through the crowd toward the starting ramp. Previously, Gibson had a key chain with the car keys.

When they lined up to start at Brescia, John pushed the starter, but the engine wouldn't start. He kept pushing and pushing it when it made a strange sound. Then a fire started in the engine compartment. Smoke came from the air scoop and paint on the aluminum hood started to bubble and peel. Fitch kept on trying to start it until finally it caught. He gunned it in neutral, which sucked the flames back into the carburetor, putting out the fire. While this was going on, Gibson was frantically looking for the key chain so he could unlock the hood.

With the fire out and the engine running, they finally arrived at the top of the ramp. They were among the last to go of the total of more than 600 competitors. Just as the sun was coming out, they plunged off the starting ramp and drove through the streets of Brescia. Soon, however, John heard a whining sound that indicated to him that there was some problem with the rear axle. Outside of town, they got up to 120 mph and the sound subsided.

But then, their drive came to a sudden halt. John remembered that "Driving through lush farm land, we came to a turn that I had to take at 80 mph. When I put on the brake, the pedal went completely to the floor. I swung the wheel and slid through the turn." It turned out the problem was a broken brake line and all the fluid had leaked out. Stopped at the side of the road, they were able to do a crude refit to the line. But when John got back into the drivers' seat and tried the brake pedal, it went all the way to the floor again. John got out and flattened the rear brake line, disabling the rear brakes. With only the front brakes operable, they started off again. But so much time had gone by that the road was no longer closed and was open again to normal traffic. Among cars, bicycles and trucks, and with the front brakes spongy, they decided the better part of valor was to give it up and return to Brescia.

Afterwards, John said he didn't find the car a very good performer as the car was too heavy for the brakes. In addition, the straight-six Nash engine didn't have a lot of power. Even so, he found it comfortable and pleasing for touring and the Pinin Farina styling attractive.

INDIANAPOLIS

Since he was a kid, John's dream was to race in the 500. After all, Indianapolis was his home town. His step-father had raced there, had toured the course with young John riding shotgun and had taken him to many of the events. Fitch had an opportunity to realize his dream during the 1953 "Month of May," as participants called it in those days. The reason was that testing, practicing and qualifying took most of the month each year for American pros.

John soon discovered what other road-racers had— including the great Juan Fangio—that driving the "Brickyard" is vastly different than competition on a road course. The basic technique is quite different. On a road course, drivers speed towards a variety of different corners, brake and drift through. At Indy, the turns are all left hand and the cars are set up to carry more weight on the right-front and left-rear wheels with much stiffer suspension. Turns are taken at high speeds with minimal drifting.

The opportunity arose when John's step-dad's friend, Indianapolis Chrysler dealer Jim ("Browny") Brown offered him a ride in the Brown Special. The car was different in some ways than most of the others. For one thing, it had an independent front suspension whereas the others had solid front axles. And the frame was made out of aluminum. This caused flexing and shuddering when going over the rough surface of the bricks.

When Fitch got to Indy he made friends with Sam Hanks. Although they didn't meet there, during the war, both Sam and

JOHN COOPER FITCH

John were pilots during WWII. John also got reacquainted with Bill Vukovich, whom he had met in Mexico during the Carrera Panamericana.

Below: The Brown Special.

The driver's test consisted in turning a number of laps at various speeds while officials looked on. After passing the test, Fitch took the Brown Special out to qualify. The best he could average was 133 mph. The minimum speed to make the field that year was 135. So Brown had Bob Sweikert give the car a try. When he returned to the pits, he suggested a number of modifications including a lower gear ratio and stiffer shocks.

With time running out for John, Sam Hanks suggested Fitch give Ray Crawford's Kurtis-Kraft a try. Ray had failed his driver's test. After doing eight laps, however, John still couldn't get to 135 mph. So ended John's Indy foray. He concluded that it would take an inordinate amount of time to learn the required technique in order to make only one race a year.

THE 1953 LE MANS

Back at home, it wasn't long before John packed enough luggage, not only for himself, but also for Elizabeth and young John and they were off to take a ship for France. Briggs Cunningham had assigned Fitch and Phil Walters to drive his new C-5R at Le Mans that June.

Left to right: Phil Walters, Briggs Cunningham and John Fitch.

Briggs had great hopes for the new car. It was 200 pounds lighter than the C-4R plus some engine modifications produced more power. Everyone on the team hoped that 1953 would be the Cunningham year at the Sarthe Circuit.

A rather large group left New York aboard the Queen Mary on May 26. John's family included Elizabeth, who was pregnant again, plus two-year old Johnny as well as both John's and Elizabeth's mothers. Others included Briggs, his wife, Lucie, and their daughters. Several mechanics, motorsports journalist Tom McCahill and Tom's dog "Joe," a black retriever, rounded out the party.

The ship landed at Cherbourg on May 31. The Fitch family had rented an apartment in Paris. Due to his drive for them earlier in the year, Rootes Motors supplied John with a Sunbeam-Talbot for the summer. When the time came, John drove the car to Le Mans. Their plan was for Elizabeth and Lucie to join them at Le Mans later in the month.

Briggs arrived with a large entourage that included a new C-5R to be driven by John Fitch and Phil Walters, a C-4R for Cunningham himself and Bill Spear, plus a C-4RK with Charles Moran and John Gordon Bennet up. They had stiff competition from some of the world's best drivers: Stirling Moss, Alberto Ascari, Juan Manuel Fangio, Mike Hawthorn, Karl Kling, Piero Taruffi and Louis Chiron, whom Fitch had met when the French champion visited with young John's family in Indianapolis. Factory teams were there in force: Jaguar, Ferrari, Porsche, Aston Martin, Allard and Alfa Romeo. The Donald Healey Motor Co. brought Austin-Healeys as well as Nash-Healeys. In addition to the scores of participants, more than 300,000 spectators showed up that year.

The weather was ideal for racing: warm and clear with only a light breeze. Sixty cars lined up along the pits with 60 drivers ready to run across the road, jump in their cars, start engines and speed off for the first lap. The cars were lined up according to their engine sizes with the largest first. The Chrysler engines sported 5.4 liters, so the Cunningham entries were two, three and four. The first car was a supercharged Talbot. The rules stated that supercharging doubles the engine capacity. The car, with 4.5 liters, had Pierre Levegh at the wheel. The Allards, with their Cadillac engines came next and so on down to the smallest cars.

Briggs had decided that Walters would take the first stint in the C-5R. He was not first away, however. Most of the European drivers didn't wear seat belts (there were no harnesses in those days). They were afraid of being trapped in a car if there was an accident; they preferred to take their chances and, perhaps, to be thrown clear. But Phil took the time to carefully fasten it before starting. Plus he didn't want to get involved in the chaotic scramble of the start.

At the end of the first lap, an Allard was leading, but Stirling Moss in a Jaguar soon passed. Walters was among the first ten. After viewing the start, John repaired to the Cunningham house trailer stocked with a plethora of food and drink. Six-month pregnant Elizabeth was there too with Lucie Cunningham and her two daughters. Lucie had even had a supply of beef ground in Paris so the Americans could enjoy hamburgers.

Soon, cars started to drop out. The first was the leading Allard and then the Hawthorn/Farina Ferrari. Fangio was next when his engine quit. Attrition was fierce as it often is at Le Mans. Of the 60 that started, only 26 lasted the 24 hours that year. When Walters passed by, one of the Cunningham mechanics noticed that Phil started bending his head down, although he was still making the same lap times. When he came in at 6:50 p.m., he had the mechanic get rid of the bug deflector, which was a plastic device intended to keep bugs from the drivers' faces. The problem was that it created an adverse current that caused the air to beat on Phil's face. The device had not been in place during practice since it had only been installed the night before the race.

John took over and, when he came to the Esses, he saw that Reg Parnell's Aston Martin had crashed. When Fitch got to the 3½-mile Mulsanne Straight, he could go 160 mph. This was very fast for an open car without wings or spoilers. After the Straight there is a kink that John took flat out when he could use the full width of the track. After the kink comes the Mulsanne Corner—actually two right turns—that required him to slow to less than 30 mph. This required hard braking.   Below: John Fitch in the C-5R.

The Cunningham cars still had drum brakes whereas the Jaguars had discs. This could have made a real difference in the final results. John's turn at the wheel had marked the approaching dusk. Later, Fitch remembered he didn't mind driving in the dark as he liked the evening air. As he became more and more comfortable with the car, his lap times kept dropping. Finally, he got the "EZ" sign from the pits.

At 10 p.m. John got the "IN" sign, came in and turned the car back over to Walters. During the stop, Fitch was told that he had moved up from ninth when he took over to fifth place. Not only that, none of the other two Cunninghams had dropped out. Rolt and Duncan held a commanding lead in the Jaguar, a lap ahead of the second-place car.

Back in the motorhome, John had a hamburger—made with French bread and butter—with Elizabeth, then dropped off to take a nap. At 1 a.m., he was awakened and told that Phil was due in shortly. So he had a cup of coffee, kissed Elizabeth and was off for his second stint. When John took over, Phil told him the brakes were fading. When John got up to speed, he found this was true, so he had to back off sooner for corners. All of a sudden, fog drifted in, covering the course so that he couldn't see even 100 yards ahead. There were no lights on the road except for the pit area.

At half distance, when dawn broke, the Fitch/Walters C-5R had advanced to third overall. After hearing the good news, John was optimistic. Suddenly, however, while he was speeding at 120 mph, the engine raced when the gear popped into neutral. Fitch soon diagnosed the cause. When turning, the centrifugal force on his body pushed him into the shift lever. So he cinched up his seatbelt, and the problem went away.

Then it was Walters turn again. At that point, only the Jaguar and a Ferrari were ahead of them. During John's stop, he learned that his good friend, Tom Cole, who was running in sixth, had crashed and died. Cole had owned the Allard in which John had won the Grand Prix of Buenos Aires.

Back behind the wheel again, the clutch in the C-5R started to slip. When this happened, Stirling Moss in his Jaguar got by. Walters took over at 11:30 a.m. and then John again at 1 p.m. Duncan Hamilton and Stirling were ahead. Just before the 4 p.m. finish, Hamilton and Fitch got into a dice. With superior power, the C-5R could out accelerate the Jaguar. But the disc brakes made the difference. As they were approaching the checkered flag, John jumped ahead. Although he was a few feet ahead, he was five laps behind. Stirling and Peter Walker finished in second, four laps behind the winner. Fitch and Walters had won their class (5-8 liters). All of the Cunninghams finished with Briggs and Bill Spear in seventh with the Charles Moran/John Gordon Bennet C-4RK in tenth. This was a sensational result for the Americans. The C-5R had covered the 2498.2 miles at 104.14 mph, more than seven miles faster than the previous year's winner. They had also set a speed record of 155 mph. This was the best result at Le Mans to date for an all-American team, one that would stand for some years to come.

When John congratulated Duncan Hamilton for his win, John said, "Dunc, whatever possessed you to race flat-out with me during the last few miles, risking your win?" Hamilton smiled and replied, "Oh, we always like to have a go, old chap!"

REIMS

While the team was in France, Briggs Cunningham decided to take on the Grand Prix of France at Reims. Reims is a city about 100 miles northeast of Paris. It is the Champagne capital of the world. In 1953, it had a population of about 150,000. The 7.8 km course is to the west of the city in a rough triangle between the small towns of Thillois, Gueux and Gayenne. Races were run clockwise on public roads. It was one of the fastest circuits ever. In 1966, Sir Jack Brabham's race average in his Brabham-Repco was 135.801 mph. Lorenzo Bandini ran the fastest lap at 141.435 mph.

Racing started there in 1925 with the Grand Prix of the Marne. The following year, a 12-hour endurance race for touring cars was added. Before WWII, it was the site of the Grands Prix of France. Formula One events were held there starting in 1953 with the last in 1966. From 1953 through 1967, the 12-Hours of Reims sports car races were held there. The course has not been used since 1967.

Briggs entered the Le Mans C-5R for Fitch and Walters with himself and Sherwood Johnston in a C-4R. Elizabeth came with John, but left young Johnny in Paris with his two grandmothers. Elizabeth had a negative feeling about the race. After taking a tour around the course, she told John she thought it was too narrow and too fast. In retrospect, perhaps John should have heeded her intuition.

The 1953 12-hour enduro started at midnight on July 3 and concluded at noon the next day. It was different than any other in that the first half was run in darkness. On July 4, the town's people, who appreciated their liberation from the Nazis less than ten years previously, set off an impressive display of fireworks in honor of the American team.

Phil Walters took the first leg, running across the road for the Le Mans start. When he turned the C-5R over to John at 3 a.m., they were second behind Umberto Maglioli's Ferrari. Although the Cunningham was heavier than the Ferrari, its engine was running strong. At maximum revs, the car would go about 156 mph which should be fast enough to win. The drive in the dark was difficult in that John had to avoid the many small, slower cars. He got a stiff neck from the force of the air over the windscreen.

As John told the rest of the story:

> *At dawn, with five hours of racing behind us, the C-5R was feeling good, getting lighter as the tanks emptied and the tires increased their bite on the road. I was able to hold the throttle wide open as I whipped under the Dunlop bridge and into the first turn. It was nearly light now; when I reached the end of that fast turn, the rear of the car suddenly broke to the outside at 130 mph. I attempted to correct, but no response. I knew I was in real trouble this time with the machine charging out of control for a ditch and the field beyond. There was a quick wrench at the safety belt as the car took its first end-over-end plunge. Each time we hit I thought that this had got to be the last one. Each impact was spine-shattering, impossibly sharp and stunning. I ducked to the side, still holding the wheel, bracing elbows against hips to stay in. Then, finally, silence. It was all over. And I was still alive!*

Fitch climbed stiffly from the twisted wreckage of the cockpit and limped to a nearby first-aid station. His injuries, miraculously, were slight, although the Cunningham was a total loss.

Back in the pits, John was told that he had taken over the lead just before the crash because the Maglioli Ferrari had been disqualified. "That was bitter news," John remarked, "but at least I had survived a really severe crash and I realized that luck was still with me." John had been worried that Elizabeth would be upset, but he found that she had slept through the whole thing.

Stirling Moss ended up winning the race with Briggs and Sherwood Johnston third in the C-4R. Originally, Cunningham had intended to keep racing in Europe, but with the C-5R gone, he gave up on the idea and returned to the U.S.

THE ALPINE RALLY

Ten days later, on July 10, 1953, Fitch was scheduled to start in the famous Alpine Rally (Rallye des Alpes Françaises) in its 16th running. As it had early in the year for the Monte Carlo, the Rootes Group contracted with John to drive a Sunbeam Alpine. The problem was that John was still recovering from his injuries. Although not very serious, they were nevertheless painful. "The slightest movement hurt and every muscle and tendon ached." Fortunately, after a few days, the throbbing pain in his temple disappeared.

After Rheims, Elizabeth and John returned to Paris. Elizabeth didn't have any qualms about the Alpine. The rally started at Marseilles, along the Côte d'Azur, the Mediterranean coast in the south of France. Fitch and Peter Collins drove down together from Paris. Fitch and Collins had co-driven a Sunbeam-Talbot in the 1952 Alpine. They hadn't been able to finish, however, when the clutch failed. Even so, they were scored 21st overall.

In 1929, the Austrian Alpine Trials, started in 1914, were reconstituted as the International Alpine Rally. The route ran across the frontiers of the Alps. It included parts of Austria, France, Germany, Italy and Switzerland. As the name implies, competitors had to contend with one mountain pass after another. It was, to say the least, difficult. The roads were the worst-paved, most devious and the steepest. It was hardly the route tourists and normal travelers usually take. From the July warmth on the Mediterranean coast, the route climbed onto bitter cold at passes, some over 9,000 feet elevation. And unlike actual open-road racing where there are no other vehicles, rally competitors had to contend with normal traffic.

Rootes had developed and entered a one-off rally car, a Sunbeam-Talbot drophead coupé, derived from the Sunbeam-Talbot 90 Saloon (sedan in American), that was entered in the 1952 Alpine. For 1953, the company made a two-seater sports roadster dubbed the Sunbeam Alpine. The car had a four-cylinder 2267cc engine and three-speeds plus overdrive gears with the shifter mounted on the column.

The Sunbeam Alpine driven by Peter Collins in 1953.

Peter Miller, an employee of Sunbeam-Talbot in England, was assigned as John's navigator. Peter was an experienced race driver in his own right. He drove for Aston Martin and won the Tourist Trophy in 1953. The two were part of the six-car Rootes team that also included Peter Collins and Stirling Moss, as well as the famous woman rally driver, Sheila Van Damm.

JOHN COOPER FITCH

In a rally, the job of the navigator is just as important as that of the driver. An exact route must be followed and timing is critical. Fitch and Miller didn't get along all that well. Peter partied a lot, taking part in as much of the night-life as possible. At a party in Marseilles the night before the start, he jumped from the quay into the harbor, a prank resulting from a dare. Rootes Team Manager Norman Gerrod, had to reprimand him after Miller dripped water on the hotel lobby floor. Originally, Peter had thought he would be a co-driver, but Fitch never trusted him at the wheel and Gerrod went along with this. At one time, John suggested Peter "try to get himself organized." After the rally was over, Miller described Fitch as, at times, being "in a foul mood" and driving along "in angry silence."

Fitch was still somewhat sore when they left Marseilles in the dark of night and headed north to Aix-en-Provence where the first control was located. (In rallying, each leg is supposed to be traveled in an exact time. Controls are spotted throughout the route where each entrant must stop to get their rally card stamped with the time.) They made their first gas stop in that most beautiful of French cities. Peter paid for the gasoline as he was in charge of finances and paperwork. They would be traveling through five different countries, each of whom had different currencies. (This was way before the Euro.) So Miller had to have a supply of these currencies. In addition, as they would cross a total of 16 borders, going through customs and immigration at each where they had to present their passports and papers for the car.

The route started at Marseilles, then to Provence, over the 7,000-foot Col d'Izoard Pass, Montgenèvre, through the Hautes Alps, Turin, Milan, Monza, the 6,180-foot Tonale Pass, Male, Bolzano, the Falzareggo Pass, Cortina, the Pordoi Pass, return to Cortina, the Gross Glockner and Gavia Passes, Munich, the Stelvio Pass, St. Moritz, Val d'Isère, the Bernina Pass, Aosta, the Petit St. Bernard Pass, Briançon, the Izoard Pass, Grasse, finish at Cannes.

Rather than recounting the entire trip, perhaps it will be more interesting to take a look at highlights that Fitch remembered. The "Circuit of the Dolomites" was a 190-mile loop from Cortina and back. It included a 30-mile time test for the climb up to the top of the Pordoi Pass. When they started out, John noticed that the car was handling badly. So he asked Peter to lean out and take a look at the tires. He saw that the left-rear wheel was shimmying. They parked and jacked up the car in order to change the wheel. While they were working, Dr. John Barker, driving another of the Sunbeams, slid across the road, hit a stone post, went end-over-end and down off the edge of the road. John ran over to take a look. What he saw was the car, upside down with the wheels still spinning. Miraculously, Dr. Barker and his navigator were uninjured and managed to crawl out of the wreck through a broken window. The Fitch/Miller Sunbeam Alpine only had two seats, so they couldn't take any passengers. Later, they found out that the car had been hoisted back onto the road. Barker and Sleep drove the wreck all the way to Cannes so they would be there for the post-Rally ceremonies and parties.

Still on the loop, when they got to Feltre, they had a problem finding a gas station. When they finally found one, they had lost some time and, in their haste, only filled ¾ of the tank. Driving fast in an effort to make up for the lost time, they ran out of gas just before Cortina. Rules allowed the competitors to carry a 5-liter can of gas. After putting the gas into the tank, they sped off to Cortina, thinking they would be late. But lo-and-behold, John had been driving so fast they arrived 14 minutes early.

After leaving Munich, they stopped in Garmisch for gas. After the German attendant had filled the tank, Miller discovered he didn't have enough marks (the German currency) to pay the bill. Not wanting to lose time changing money at a bank, Peter stuffed a wad of Italian lire, Swiss francs and Austrian schillings into the bewildered attendant's hands.

Switzerland had some very low speed limits, only 30 mph in places. And they insisted on strict enforcement, even on rally participants. Swiss police would even phone ahead, warning cops in town when rally cars were approaching. Taking Swiss laws into consideration, Fitch almost crept along, managing not to be stopped. Those who were stopped had to proceed directly to the local justice and pay a fine before being allowed to go on.

When they reached the end at Cannes, they found out that they had driven the entire route on the required schedule, having not lost any points. They finished with a perfect score and won a Coupe des Alpes (Alpine Cup). John was the very first American to achieve this feat. Out of 102 starters they finished 20th overall with a sixth-place class (2000 to 2600cc) finish.

The awards banquet was held in the Hôtel Carlton. To the surprise of the officials, an unprecedented total of 25 cars won a Coupe des Alpes. There weren't a sufficient number of cups, so some winners had to receive theirs in the mail.

Out of the six Sunbeam Alpine starters, four won cups including Sheila Van Damm, who was also awarded a Coupe des Dames. She was the only woman winner that year and only the second one ever to do so. Stirling Moss drove the Alpine in a Sunbeam for Rootes in 1952, 1953 and 1954. In all three, he was able to finish without penalty and was awarded a Coupe de Alpes each year. Having lost its Esso sponsorship, the last Alpine was held in 1971. Nevertheless, in its day, the Alpine had great prestige in the world of motorsports.

JOHN'S FIRST GRAND PRIX

Back in Paris, the Fitch family that included John, Elizabeth, Johnny plus the two grandmothers, moved out of their small, crowded apartment and rented a house in nearby Neuilly, only a short distance from Paris. There, they settled in for the summer in what Elizabeth said was "an utterly charming place." Young Johnny climbed in a chestnut tree in the front yard. The house was convenient in that Fitch had some additional rides in Europe. The first was John's first in a Grand Prix.

John had received an offer to drive for John Cooper in one of the team's Formula 2 cars. All of his expenses would be paid and, in addition, he was to get a small remuneration (80,000 French francs, about $230). In spite of the meager fee, John agreed to come because it was his first chance to drive a formula car in a grand prix.

The race was the 1953 5th Grand Prix du Lac for Formula 2 cars. It was at the Aix-les-Bains, a lake about 40 miles from Geneva. The course was a temporary one called the Circuit du Lac d'Aix-les-Bains (the lake race track). About 1½ miles long, it was, as its name implies, along the lake, then through the small resort town, past houses, shops and docked sailboats. Races were held there from 1949 through 1960.

The car John drove was a Cooper-Bristol. John Cooper and his partner, Owen Maddock, formed the Cooper Car Co. in 1947. Based at Surbiton, UK, they made a large number of Formula 3 (500cc) racing cars. The Formula 2 Cooper-Bristol was their first attempt at a larger car. The power plant was the venerable 2-liter, 6-cylinder Bristol engine that produced almost 150 bhp. It was derived from the very successful thirties-era BMW engine that powered the famous 328 BMW roadster. The engine design was acquired by the British Bristol Aeroplane Company in reparations following WWII. Perhaps its best-known use was in the AC Bristol sports car that enjoyed many racing successes, both in Europe and the U.S. When the Bristol company stopped making the engines, the AC Company partnered with Carroll Shelby to make the Shelby Cobra using the small-block Ford V8.

When Fitch fitted himself into the cockpit, he soon discovered that it wasn't designed to accommodate someone of John's height. It was a tight squeeze with his knees wedged against the instrument panel. Problems arose even on the first lap of practice. The engine cut out on tight turns and it failed to rev for downshifting. Then he couldn't get it into either first or second. After the Cooper mechanics worked on the car, John took it out again for more practice.

The field included some top international stars. Maurice Trintignant, Harry Schell and Jean Behra were in Gordinis, Lance Macklin and Peter Collins in an HWM and Onofre Marimon in a Maserati. John's was the sole Cooper.

John Fitch in the Formula 2 Cooper-Bristol.

July 26, 1953 was the day of the race. On the warm-up lap, the engine misfired again fouling the plugs. After John came in to change them, Team Manager Alan Brown shook his head and remarked, "It looks bad. Just run as long as you can." Fitch decided his strategy would be to keep going as long as he could, avoid, if possible, making any pit stops and try to finish. This way he might have a chance to place.

The race was run in two heats. When the first heat started, the Cooper misfired and John was away in last place. The team didn't have any alternate gears, so Alan had smaller tires mounted on the rear in order to reduce the gear ratio. The problem was that this reduced road adhesion. The result was that the car didn't behave the same way it had in practice. So John stayed in last and, when lapped, tried to stay out of the way. As he was passing John, Peter Collins slipped on a patch of oil and slid into a row of hay bales. A few laps later, he got back on the road and passed John again. Finally, it ended with Jean Behra the winner in one hour, 11 minutes and 34 seconds. Collins was fifth, followed by Harry Schell and then last-place Fitch about a minute behind Behra. John's finishing position was eighth. Harry Schell had set the fastest lap at one minute and 20 seconds going 108 kph. Three cars had failed to finish including the Marimon Maserati that crashed and the Trintignant Gordini that caught fire.

Nine cars lined up to start the second heat. After about three laps, the Bristol engine began to run much better and John felt that he had a chance for a good finish. At the end, it was Elie Boyol in an OSCA, Louis Rosier in a Ferrari, Lance Macklin in an HWM and John Fitch in the Cooper. The others failed to finish due to various mechanical problems. So John was a very creditable fourth, only a minute or so behind the OSCA. After it was over, most of the drivers and crew members changed into swim suits and headed for the beach.

BACK TO THE RING

After only a few days with his family at their rented house near Paris, Fitch decided he wanted to take in the 1953 Grand Prix of Germany that would be held on August 2. Originally, Briggs had planned to enter his Cunningham team in one of the races held the same weekend as the GP. But due to the loss of the C-5R at Rheims, Briggs changed his mind. Even without the Cunningham, John hoped he could snag a ride with Porsche. So before leaving, he wired Ferry Porsche that he would be available.

Fitch hitched a ride to the Nur-burgring with his friend (and mine), the eminent motorsports-journalist Bernard Cahier.

My portrait of Bernard Cahier.

When they arrived, John found Porsche Team Manager Huschke von Hanstein in the garage area. Herr Porsche had told von Hanstein that Fitch was coming and was available to drive in the production-car event that would be held on Saturday, August 1. Huschke said that all of the cars had been assigned, but that per-haps Gilberte Thirion, a top woman driver, would agree to let John take her Porsche. When she pulled into the pit after a practice ses-sion, John approached her feeling "something like a villain" as he remembered. "By all means," she said, "take it. It has been raining and I don't like to race in the rain."

The Porsche coupé (above) was as he remembered from his previous drive on the Ring in 1952. He knew it would be well prepared and reliable. After six laps of practice, Fitch brought the car up to the pre-grid in preparation for the start. John was about in the middle of the pack in between two other Porsches. When the flag fell, all got away in a tightly paced group. When they approached a tight corner, two cars ahead of John spun out, blocking the road. Fitch was going too fast to brake and it was too late to try to dodge around them. Miraculously, just as he approached the still spinning cars, a small gap opened between them and he was able to slip through, in the clear and untouched.

As John went along, he saw a maroon Porsche coupé some 300 yards or so ahead. So he concentrated on catching it. When he passed the front straight by the stands, one of the Porsche mechanics held up five fingers, meaning Fitch was in fifth place. He knew that if he could pass the maroon Porsche, he would be in fourth with at least a chance to finish in the money. Eventually, he was only a few yards behind as they came to a fast bend going about 75 mph. The maroon Porsche failed to make the corner, shot straight off the road and into a field of parked spectator cars. So now he was in fourth.

As he went along, John noticed a number of competitors parked at the side of the road. He hoped that at least one was a car that had been ahead of him. With nobody in sight either ahead or behind, he settled down to a steady pace. To be in the money, he had to finish. On the last lap, he noticed one of the top Porsche drivers walking on the road back to the pits. As it turned out, that driver had been ahead of John, so when the checkered flag fell, Fitch took third overall. When he returned after his cool-off lap, both Ferry Porsche and von Hanstein offered congratulations for a more than creditable drive. John was happy to have done so well on the world's most difficult and demanding purpose-built race track.

After less than a month back with the family, John was off to Northern Ireland for the 1953 Tourist Trophy, a part of the FIA World Sports Car Championship. Fitch had secured a ride with the Frazer-Nash team in one of their Frazer-Nash Le Mans Mk IIs. He was teamed with Peter Wilson, a Brit. The race took place on September 5 on 7½ miles of open road near Dunrod. The event was a long-distance one for 111 laps. Unfortunately, after 53 laps, one of the wheels on the Fitch/Wilson Mk II fell off, so they failed to finish. John's friend, Peter Collins and his co-driver, Pat Griffith, won after 8½ hours in an Aston Martin DB3S. Afterwards, some felt it was Peter's very best drive. Another DB3S was second and a Frazer-Nash with Ken Wharton and Ernie Robb driving was third.

MONZA

Fitch had been offered a test drive in a Formula One Maserati, so he left Northern Ireland and went directly to Monza, Italy. He arrived only a few days before the Grand Prix was to take place on September 13, 1953. On his first day, there was only time for four laps. He found the famous course fast and exciting. Even though Fitch did some good laps in the A6GCM Maserati, the problem was that the team had a full roster that included Fangio, Gonzales, Bonetto and Marimon, all top drivers. Unless there was an unforeseen circumstance, it was unlikely John would get a seat.

Even though a Maserati ride didn't work out, all was not lost, however, for John at the 1953 Grand Prix of Italy. When his friend, Lance Macklin, pointed out to John Heath that Fitch had turned some good laps in a Maserati, he got a seat in an HWM-Alta. It was to be his first chance to compete in Formula One. That year, Formula One races were run under Formula Two rules, meaning that the engine sizes couldn't be larger than two liters.

HW Motors brought three cars to Monza. One was for Macklin with another for Yves Giraud Cabantous. This left a spare car that was assigned to Fitch. Hersham and Walton Motors (HWM) is located at Walton-on-Thames, England. Starting in 1950, the company constructed Formula Two cars and competed in the series. They employed 150 bhp 2-liter Alta engines. The car weighed in at only 1,230 pounds. When Formula One rules limited engines to 2-liters, HWM competed in the World Championship series. Although they had some top drivers—including Stirling

JOHN COOPER FITCH

Moss and Peter Collins—the best an HWM-Alta did in Formula One was a fifth at the 1952 Belgian GP.

The HWM team at Monza: John Fitch, Stirling Moss and crew.

John's HWM was the best placed of the team on the starting grid. But when the flag fell, Fitch was delayed by the car in front of him—Prince Bira's Maserati—balked. Finally he got away and was turning some decent laps when the engine cut out and he had to come into the pits. John Heath wrenched off the accelerator linkage, welded a break and refitted it, all in less than five minutes. Out on the track again, a fuel line started to spray his face with alcohol, so back into the pits. Finally, after 14 laps, the engine seized and that was that. The engine in the Lance Macklin HWM gave up after only six laps.

Meanwhile, the 80-lap race settled down to a contest between Ferrari and Maserati, an epic battle of champions. John and Lance went up to the "Curva Grande" (Grand Curve) to watch. Fangio in the Maserati made a bad start, so Alberto Ascari in a Ferrari took the lead. For most of the race, the three champions were neck and neck: Ascari, Fangio, and Giuseppe Farina (Ferrari). Going into the last corner of the last lap, Ascari and Farina were side by side. Ascari spun and Farina went off the course. Then Marimon, who had nowhere else to go, hit Ascari. Fangio squeezed through the wreckage to win the race with Nino Farina 1½ seconds behind. John's teammate, Giraud-Cabantous, finished in 15th, 13 laps behind the leader.

After the race, two Americans, who were strangers to John, approached him in the pits and introduced themselves. It turned out that both were in the movie business working on a film about racing. Julian Blaustein was the producer and Charlie Kaufman, the writer. They planned to make a production for 20th Century-Fox, based on a novel, *The Racer*, written by a driver, Hans Reusch. Their problem was that Monza was the very first road race either of them had ever seen. The two were interested in talking with Fitch about it since he was one of the few Americans then racing in Europe. John suggested they get together in Paris after he had returned home.

A few weeks later, Blaustein, Kaufman and the writer Hans Reusch met with Fitch. Elizabeth, who was eight months pregnant, accompanied John. Originally, the plan was for Reusch to participate in the production. But the previous month, he had survived a serious crash in his Ferrari during a race. He had rather painful in-juries and couldn't help as a driver with the movie.

The plan was to make a spectacle in wide-screen Cinemas-cope and Technicolor with a lot of action and violence. The budget was $2,500,000. That was lots of money in those days. Although John was asked to consider being the technical director, no final plans were made and they agreed to meet again in the U.S. later in the year.

BACK TO THE U.S.

There were no more races in Europe for John in 1953, so it was time to return to the U.S. When they arrived, Elizabeth gave birth to their second son, Christopher, on October 23. Fitch had agreed to drive for Briggs at Turner Air Force Base near Albany, Georgia. The event was scheduled for October 25, so John had to leave right after Christopher was born.

The Turner AFB race was called "Sowega," because of its location in SOuth-WEst GA (Georgia). Briggs entered four Cunninghams, John Fitch, Phil Walters, Charlie Moran and Briggs himself. Fitch drove the C-5 in two races. The first was a preliminary event, The King George Cup, which John won. Competition for the main event—the Strategic Air Power Race—was tough. Phil Walters was in a second Cunningham, Phil Hill, Bill Spear and Bill Lloyd in Ferraris with Karl Kling and Huschke von Hanstein in Porsches. Zora Arkus-Duntov, with whom John was to later interact, was driving an Allard. The Cunningham team strategy was for Walters to set an initial fast pace with Fitch saving his tires in the corners. Then, when Phil had to pit for tires, John was to take the lead.

It didn't work, however. Hill and Spear passed John right away and started contesting the lead with Walters. By lap 14, Spear and Walters were battling, but both Porsches and the Hill Ferrari had dropped out with mechanical troubles. At half distance, Walters came in for gas and tires, leaving Spear in front with Fitch in second, more than two minutes behind. Towards the end, Fitch started to narrow the gap. When it was reduced to 26 seconds, the Cunningham's brakes locked up and John came to a complete stop. After he got going again, but without brakes, he knew there was no hope of catching Spear. And that's the way it ended. Bill Spear in first, John Fitch second, Phil Hill third and Jim Kimberly fourth. Fitch had not had to pit for tires and, at the end, they were completely worn out and probably couldn't have made more than another lap or two.

The final SCCA National of 1953—the Orange Empire National Sports Car Races—was at March Air Force Base near Riverside, California on November 8. It was the first time the Los Angeles Region of the SCCA had hosted a major event. Some interesting personalities showed up. Actor Keenan Wynn drove a Kurtis for Frank Kurtis and George Barris drove a Jaguar. Riddelle (Rocket) Gregory won the Novice Race in his brother's C-Type Jaguar. Ignacio Lozano, publisher of the Los Angeles Spanish-language daily newspaper, reported on the event for the SCCA magazine, *Sports Car*. Ken Miles won the under-1500cc event in his first MG special, R-1.

Fitch got to California on November 5 in order to meet with Julian Blaustein about the movie. They talked about it that day, but the production was still in the "uncertain" category. The next day, Charlie Kaufman took John on a tour of the 20th Century-Fox lot. They agreed that if the film was actually produced, John would be on board.

Briggs entered himself, Phil Walters and John Fitch in C-4Rs. Some other top drivers were there for the main event: Phil Hill, Jim Kimberly, Sherwood Johnston, Bill Spear, Sterling Edwards and Jack McAfee, all in Ferraris, plus 1952 Indy-winner Troy Ruttman in a Kurtis and Masten Gregory in a C-Type Jaguar.

Before 70,000 spectators, Fitch took the lead on the 15th of the 50-lap, 175-mile race and continued in front for the balance of the contest. His average speed was 87.62 mph and at one time, he was clocked at 146 mph on the back straight. Briggs finished second followed by Bill Spear, Masten Gregory and Jim Kimberly. Ruttman, who had been running in fourth, threw a rod in the Mercury engine towards the end and failed to finish.

John was presented with the trophy (above) by actor Dick Powell while actress June Allyson gave Fitch the traditional kiss. It was a plus for me as I met John after the race, took his picture and shook his hand. Little did we know then that we would enjoy a lifetime of friendship.

MEXICO AGAIN

John's 1953 racing year wasn't quite over just yet. His friend, Carl Kiekhaefer, asked him to drive a Chrysler New Yorker in Mexico. The day after March Field—October 9th—Fitch flew from LAX to Mexico City. The Chrysler didn't arrive until October 16th, so John spent the time going over parts of the road that would be the route for the race. He logged his observations on a tape recorder and each evening transcribed them onto notes for use during the event. Kiekhaefer had entered four New Yorkers with drivers Frank Menendez, Bob Korf, Reg McKee and John.

'53 Chrysler New Yorker

Soon after Fitch and his navigator, Bud Boile, set off from Tuxtla Gutiérrez the torque converter in the Chrysler transmission split, so they had to proceed at a much reduced speed.

The plan was to try to reach Oaxaca where repairs could be attempted. After a while, they came upon Jack Ensley by the side of the road. He was driving his own 500K Kurtis with a Cadillac engine. Jack had run out of fuel. So John gave him a ride. Bill Vukovich became the next passenger and the New Yorker's backseat was full. Bill had been driving a Lincoln Capri when the transmission failed.

As the car load was proceeding along the long Tehuantepec straightaway, they saw skid marks stretching for hundreds of yards before leaving the road. It turned out to be Antonio Stagnoli's 375 Ferrari Mille Miglia. With the Ferrari doing 180 mph or so, one of the front tires blew out. After going off the road, the car rolled a number of times and then caught fire. All four in the New Yorker stopped and got out to see if they could help. But Stagnoli had already lost his life.

After they reached Oaxaca, officials announced that the Kiekhaefer New Yorker had failed to make the first leg in the minimum amount of time allowed, so they were officially out of the race. In fact, none of the Kiekhaefer New Yorkers were able to finish. The Menendez car was also over the time limit, McKee was in an accident and Korf was a DNF. John told his friend Carl that in the future, he should provide cars that would stay together. Apparently Kiekhaefer took the advice to heart. During the next few years, he had a team of Chryslers that dominated stock-car racing.

Not in contention by then for the championship, Mercedes Benz didn't enter a team in the Carrera Panamericana in 1953. Their top driver, Juan Manuel Fangio won in a Lancia followed by Piero Taruffi in another Lancia. Chuck Stevenson won the stock-car class in a Lincoln with Walt Faulkner second, also in a Lincoln. Fangio covered the 1,912 miles in 18 hours and 11 minutes averaging 105.149 mph. The race started with 182 cars leaving Tuxtla Gutiérrez, but only 60 made it to the finish at Ciudad Juárez. The race was marred by the death of not only Stagnoli, but also Felice Bonetto.

Speed Age magazine selected John Fitch as the "Sports Car Driver of the Year" for 1953. All in all, John had a very successful year having won Sebring and placing third at Le Mans. He also won three SCCA races and placed in a number of others.

JOHN COOPER FITCH

Fitch returned to his home in Stamford from Mexico. His next commitment was to drive the 12-Hours of Sebring for Briggs Cunningham. It wouldn't take place until March, so John looked forward to spending some quality time with his family. He wanted to get acquainted with his new son, Christopher, who was only two months old. With Connecticut in the depths of winter, John promised Elizabeth that they would spend three months in Florida. Just before they left, Fitch talked on the phone with Julian Blaustein at 20th Century Fox in Hollywood. Blaustein offered, and John accepted, a salary of $350 (more than $3,000 in today's money) a week to serve as technical adviser for the upcoming production of *The Racers*. Shooting was to take place in Europe during 1954.

After they arrived in Florida, Briggs Cunningham prevailed on John to drive a 2.9 Ferrari at an SCCA race at MacDill Air Force Base near Tampa, Florida on January 31, 1954. Jim Kimberly won the main event in a 4.5 Ferrari with John third overall and first in Class D Modified. This was the first SCCA National of the year; 1954 was the first year that SCCA awarded championships in each class. Previously only the overall winner was the champion.

Briggs entered the 1954 12-Hours of Sebring with John Fitch and Phil Walters in a 4.5-liter 375 Ferrari plus himself and Sherwood Johnston in a Cunningham. Walters took the first leg, but had to pit on lap 6 with fouled spark plugs. It took five minutes to change them as there were 12 in the Ferrari engine. Ascari, Fangio and Taruffi led the race in Lancias. Soon, however, both Fangio and Ascari suffered mechanical problems and were out. In the third hour, John took over for Phil and, at the half way point, advanced into second overall behind the Taruffi/Manzon Lancia. He was able to hold that position for another hour, but then the Ferrari brakes started to fade and Fitch had to downshift early in order to slow the car for corners. On lap 104, the engine failed and that was that for the Fitch/Walters entry. Cunningham had a surprise victory however. He had entered Stirling Moss and Bill Lloyd in a small

OSCA MT4 with a 4-cylinder 1491cc engine. The cars were known as "giant killers" and this one surely lived up to its name. Moss and Lloyd won overall in an upset. Two other OSCAs were among the top five finishers. Years later Moss acquired an MT4 that he campaigned in a number of historic races. He said it was one of his favorite cars.

LIVING IN EUROPE DURING 1954

Cunningham had entered Fitch in the June Le Mans as well as the July Rheims 12 hour. In addition, John had to be on hand during the filming of *The Racers*. So right after Sebring, he went to Europe in order to find a place for the family to live. It took some time, but eventually he found just what he was looking for: a large house—the Villa Clerici—in northern Italy near Lake Como. Subsequently, Elizabeth and their sons joined him and they settled in. The Fitch family shared the villa with the Masten Gregory family which included his wife, three children and their nursemaids. In addition, there was an Italian cook and gardener plus a German housemaid. Life in the villa could be confusing as none of the Americans spoke Italian nor did the Italians speak any English. Evelyn, the housemaid, spent a lot of time translating.

Soon it was time for the June 12-13 Le Mans. Briggs entered John and Phil Walters in a new 4.5-liter 375MM Ferrari (right). He also entered Bill Spear and Sherwood Johnston, plus himself and John Gordon,  in Cunningham C-4Rs. The Fitch/Walters Ferrari was never a serious threat and, after 120 laps, retired with a mechanical problem. Froilián Gonzales and Maurice Trintigant won in a 4.9-liter 375 Ferrari with Duncan Hamilton and Tony Rolt second in a D-Type.

Spear and Johnston made a good showing in third with Briggs and John Gordon in fifth.

Afterwards, Briggs remarked to John that "Our cars just can't stand up against the kind of opposition we face out there. Looks like this is the last time I'll be taking them to Le Mans." Cunningham knew he had done as much as possible with them.

Next on the agenda was the 12-Hours of Rheims. Briggs had kept the Le Mans cars in France, so he entered John and Phil in a C-4R. It would be the last time Fitch would pilot a Cunningham in anger. The pair managed a sixth overall. The Cunningham team returned to the U.S. while John started a new career in the movies.

MAKING *THE RACERS*

The Racers is a film about professional road racing in Europe. The 88 minute motion picture was produced and released by 20th Century Fox in May 1955. Made in Cinemascope and De Luxe color, it was directed by Henry Hathaway, staring Kirk Douglas and Bella Darvi with Gilbert Roland, Cesar Romero and Lee J. Cobb. The story was based on a novel, *The Racer*, by former race-driver Hans Reusch.

The plot involves a race-driver, Gino (played by Douglas) and a ballerina, Nicole (played by Darvi) in a romance. After winning the Mille Miglia, Gino is hired by a team managed by Maglio (played by Lee J. Cobb). Carlos Chavez (played by Cesar Romero) is also on the team. Gino is seriously injured in a crash after which Nicole persuades doctors not to amputate Ginos' leg. Carlos is about to retire and Maglio instructs Gino to let Carlos win his last race.

But Gino wins anyway. And so on. Although the plot is somewhat contrived, the racing scenes are authentic and the film is well worth seeing.

John Fitch and Baron Emmanuel "Tulo" de Graffenreid were "technical consultants," but ended up doing most of the stunt driving and serving as doubles for the actors in the racing scenes. John was previously acquainted with Tulo, who was a Swiss who had recently retired from racing. One of his important talents was that he was fluent in French, German, Italian and English. The two worked well together.

The story was about a racing team that fielded fictional cars called "Buranos." A requirement was that they not look like any existing cars. So John, working with some friends at Pinin Farina in Torino, designed unique bodies—a Formula One and a sports car—that could be made by altering cars that they would acquire for the film. During that time, Tulo roamed around Europe to find suitable machines. First, he found three Grand Prix Maseratis he was able to buy from an estate. Then he bought a HWM-Alta from its Swiss owner. It was similar to the car Fitch had raced at Monza in 1953. In addition, he bought three Ferrari sports cars. After the cars were delivered, they were farmed out to various Italian body shops for reworking and reshaping.

At a meeting with the director, Henry Hathaway, John and Tulo were cautioned that the cars would have to be shipped to Hollywood after location filming in order to shoot close-ups. After that first encounter, Hathaway spent most of the time in the Hollywood studio while Bob Snody directed all the European racing scenes. As a matter of fact, the stars never set foot in Europe.

The film was to open showing a sports-car race at Monte Carlo. Tulo knew Prince Rainier and was able to arrange for the shoot. (The Prince, as we all know, married actress Grace Kelly in 1956.) Fitch's old friend, Louis Chiron, also acquainted with Rainier, was employed to help with arrangements such as the construction of pits and grandstands. The city was made to look as it did during an actual Grand Prix.

The first scene shows our hero, Gino (Douglas), in practice when a dog runs in front of his car and, in order to avoid the dog, wrecks the car. Fitch doubled for Douglas for the filming. Driving the HWM, he swerved to avoid the dog and "crashed" into some hay bales (below).

It was shot over and over. In one, the camera car took the place of the HWM. In addition, the sports-car "race" was filmed on the Grand Prix course. Before the accident, Gino had been doing so well that he had turned times equal to a factory Burano. So Gino is offered a seat on the team.

Next, they shot scenes that were supposedly part of the Mille Miglia. While passing another Burano, Gino grazes an arch and tears through a village. Hitting the arch is the problem. The actual arch was solid concrete. So they lined it with soft and light plaster. It was decided that John would do the hitting. To simulate the hit, Fitch bolted a short piece of iron with a hook on the end to the side of the car. Just before the arch and going at a good clip, John turned the wheel toward the arch at the last moment. There was a loud thump, a shower of debris and Fitch and his actor navigator burst through. When they stopped, they found a crumpled fender and a gouge on the side of the car, all easily repaired. And the director was happy with the first take, so another was not required.

There were some other scenes that were taken with Fitch and de Graffenreid driving as doubles for the actors. In one, Tulo, this time doubling for Douglas, is involved in a serious accident. He is supposed to go off the road, through a wood fence at Spa, into a stand of trees and explode. The fence was made of balsa wood and the incident was staged successfully.

A number of scenes were shot at actual races. Some of those who were talked into taking part included Fangio, Ascari, Villoresi and Harry Schell among others. Finally, all the work in Europe was done. Although it was sometimes a difficult job, John said he enjoyed himself. The family stayed through the winter at their rented villa. During the winter, they moved to Lugano, Switzerland having rented an old house. They would be there for the next 11 months.

John Fitch became the only American member of the Mercedes Benz racing team during 1955. He joined some of the world's greatest drivers including Juan Manuel Fangio and Stirling Moss. John was slated to drive in the Mille Miglia, Le Mans, the Tourist Trophy and the Targa Florio. It was to be a year of not only triumph, but also tragedy.

In December 1954, Fitch drove to Stuttgart with journalist Gunther Moltar. The purpose of the trip was to talk about the upcoming season with Mercedes Benz Team Manager Alfred Neubauer. During the war Moltar flew a German Focke-Wulfe ME 109 against American P-51s, a plane that Fitch had flown. During the drive, the two compared dates to see if their paths might have crossed. They hadn't, but they came close.

During the meeting in Neubauer's office in Daimler-Benz headquarters, Moltar translated for Fitch and Neubauer. First, they discussed the Mille Miglia and Neubauer asked John about his previous experiences on the route. John said he had been over it four times, but Gunther translated it as five and Neubauer was impressed. One of the Mercedes Benz top drivers, Karl Kling, had only been over it four times. Fitch was assigned a production 300 SL. The other members of the team would drive 300 SLRs.

THE 1955 MILLE MIGLIA

The 1955 Mille Miglia Mer-
cedes Benz team consisted of ten cars.
Four 300 SLRs were in the Sports Rac-
ing Class with World Champion Juan
Fangio, Stirling Moss, Karl Kling and
Hans Herrmann driving. There were
three production 300 SLs in the Gran
Tourismo Class, one driven by John
Fitch, plus three diesel-powered 180Ds
in the Sedan Class. Fitch was the only

American on the team and, as a matter of fact, the only American
driver in the 1955 Mille Miglia.

The team arrived two months before the event and all practiced extensively. Kling did some 30,000 miles. Fitch had made
arrangements with his English journalist friend, Denis Jenkinson,
to be the navigator. He felt that "Jenks," as he was called, would be
an important asset in that Jenkinson had an extensive and intimate
knowledge of the course. In addition, Jenks had been a motorcycle
racer with an important familiarity with motorsports competition.

In the usual course of events, the navigator would write extensive notes while practicing. Then, during the race, he would tell
the driver what was coming up next. The course, as its name sug-
gests, was 1,000 miles with a myriad of hazards and 2,987 turns
going from Brescia via Ravenna and Ancona to Rome, then via
Florence through Tuscany and back to Brescia.

JOHN COOPER FITCH

Fitch came up with the idea of having the navigator's notes written on a roll of paper that could be mounted in a box with a take-up reel that could be wound slowly ahead, revealing the transcribed notes in order as they progressed.

John's plan regarding Jenks however, didn't pan out. Stirling Moss decided he wanted to have an all-English team. Even though Jenks had been previously scheduled to ride with Fitch, Stirling prevailed on Neubauer to make the change. So Jenks went to Fitch and explained the decision. John remarked that he didn't have a prayer of scoring an overall victory in the stock 300 SL whereas Moss in the SLR could very well win. "Go and join Stirling," John said, "and good luck to you both."

Denis Jenkinson and Stirling Moss

Jenks took the paper-roll idea with him with John's blessing. "Jenks and I made the actual roll-map device," Moss said. The paper turned out to be some 18 feet long. Years later, Stirling acknowledged that John had invented the box.

To replace Jenks, Fitch was assigned a German journalist, Kurt Gesell (right). Gesell worked for a large photo magazine in Hamburg, *Hearing and Seeing* (translated), equivalent to *People* magazine. He had been assigned to cover the race firsthand. Although he could speak some English, he had never had any previous exposure to motor racing. So, for all intents and purposes, John ran the race without a lot of assistance. Fitch and Gesell arrived in Brescia a week before the race.

They set out to drive the course in a 180D Mercedes sedan after going over the route twice through traffic and at a moderate pace. Afterwards, Kurt said, "John, I'm amazed, I don't see how you could have possibly driven any faster." Fitch knew that Gesell was due for a rude awakening on race day. The 1955 Mille Miglia was Kurt's first and, and it turned out, his last race.

John Fitch posed for publicity photos with his car before the start.

Their 300 SL arrived at Brescia two days before the race. When John took it out for a short run, he found out that at full throttle, it pulled to the right. At that point, there was very little time to fix anything. The engineer, Rudi Uhlenhaut, took a look and found that the rear tires were different sizes. So after a tire change, everything checked out.

On the morning of the race, the entrants were set off at one-minute intervals. Fitch was scheduled start at 4:17 a.m. Each car was numbered according to the start time, so the 300 SL had 417 painted on its sides and hood.

JOHN COOPER FITCH

John and Kurt got up a little after 2 a.m. They got a caffè latte at a small shop, and then went to the garage to warm up the engine. When John gunned it, he heard a strange whirring noise. To his relief, after the oil warmed up, the sound went away.

Just before the starting time, they drove through the crowded streets towards the flag-draped grandstands and the floodlit ramp. Neubauer had John shut off the engine to prevent the spark plugs from fouling and they were pushed through into line behind #416, an Alfa Romeo. Finally, it was their turn; the flag dropped and they rolled off the ramp and onto the dark city streets. There were crowds everywhere, so John proceeded at a sedate pace until they reached the outskirts.

On the open road, John brought the revs up to 6,000 rpm in top gear, going over 150 mph when they came to a cobblestoned straight. Soon though, they had to slow down for the first little village where they caught and passed the Alfa Romeo that had started one minute beforehand. Back up to speed, they passed several more cars and skirted the southern tip of Lake Garda. The congested waterfront town of Peschiera required very cautious driving.

Soon after dawn, they drove through Verona, the first large city on the route. Now that it was light, some of the smaller cars that had already broken down could be seen at the side of the road as well as some that had been in accidents. Since there were few villages on the stretch to Vicenza, they made good time. In short order, they passed through Padova, Rovigo, Ferrara and to the control at Ravenna where their route-card was stamped. John recalled that Ravenna was where a scene for *The Racers* had been filmed.

In order for John to take a drink, a rubber hose had been attached to a thermos. But while drinking from the hose, John had dropped it when steering through a blind corner. Consequently, all the water had siphoned out and the thermos was empty. Not having anything to drink made him even thirstier.

Taking the flag for the control point at Ravenna.

After going over bridges in Rimini and onto a winding road, the car finally got up to speed again. But over 5,000 rpm, the engine started to cut out. Much to John's relief, when he switched on the auxiliary fuel pump, it ran smoothly. Leaving Ancona, the road ran along beside the Adriatic Sea. At Pescara, they stopped at the refueling station where there was a lot of confusion because 417 wasn't expected to arrive so soon. Back on the road, the engine started to miss again. With the extra fuel pump already working, there was not much that could be done other than hope it didn't get worse.

It had been cool during the night and early morning, but then it started to get really hot, particularly in the enclosed 300 SL cockpit. The second control stop was at Pescara where their card was stamped again. There was a Mercedes Benz service depot in Pescara, so they raced to the blue flag with the three-pointed star waving in the breeze. After water and a ham and cheese sandwich was passed through the car window, off they went. From practicing, John knew there was a bridge to cross in Pescara.

JOHN COOPER FITCH

But John had to slam on the brakes because the exit from the bridge was barricaded. He found that the course had been changed to cross the river at another bridge. Anxious to make up for the lost time, he crossed the second bridge too fast. At the other side, he slid into a curb, hitting the left rear tire.

Leaving Pescara, it was 8:30 a.m. At that point, they had covered some 400 miles with a better than 100 mph average speed. Then, however, the engine started to cut off again. The hope was that the problem could be fixed at the next stop in Rome where there was another Mercedes Benz depot. There was a narrow Bailey bridge in Popoli that had to be negotiated with extreme caution. The bridge had been built by the U.S. Army Corps of Engineers during WWII. It was narrow with loose planks that rattled.

The Bailey bridge built by the U.S. Army.

The road opened up and they took a series of curves at over 90 mph. In the hills outside Rome, the road became narrower and they had to slow down. In the city itself, there was a nightmare of blind curves and crowds of spectators. The control was beneath a red Mille Miglia banner where they got their card stamped.

Then they went to the Mercedes Benz depot to refuel. There wasn't time to do anything about the high-speed missing, so they went on at a reduced pace.

The Rome-Siena-Florence-Bologna section was the most difficult as well as the most decisive part of the course. Most of the roads were second-rate and there was a series of rough mountain passes. At the Siena control point, they were told they were a minute behind their class leader, Olivier Gendebien in a privately-entered 300 SL. As the Fitch engine lost power after 5,000 rpm, they were concerned that Gendebien would pull even farther ahead. Nevertheless, John was doing all he could to make up the time difference. But at Bologna, they were a minute and 20 seconds behind. On the fast stretch from Bologna to Brescia, they lost 20 mph of the top speed due to the engine miss.

The end of the race; John Fitch taking the checkered flag.

Finally, Brescia lay ahead and the crowds at each side of the road grew larger and larger. After passing the checkered flag, they stopped at the final control point.

JOHN COOPER FITCH

Emerging from the Gullwing's doors, they were greeted by back-thumpings and shouted congratulations by Neubauer and Uhlenhaut. Now they had to wait to see how Gendebien would do as he had started 11 minutes after Fitch and Gesell. Their hopes rose higher and higher as the minutes went by and no Gendebien. If he were to arrive more than 11 minutes behind, the class win would be theirs. Actually, Gendebien arrived 17 minutes later. It turned out that he had gone off the road, bending the body into a wheel which required a six-minute tire change.

Team Manager Alfred Neubauer had hoped that a production 300 SL might finish as high as tenth overall. John Fitch was fifth overall and first in class. There were 533 cars entered in the race with 60 in the class. The only cars ahead of John were Stirling Moss and Juan Fangio in 300 SLRs, Umberto Maglioli in a Ferrari and Francesco Giardini in a Maserati.

Moss set a record of 10 hours, 7 minutes and 48 seconds over the 1,000 miles. "It was my greatest drive," he said. Fitch was less than an hour and a half behind Stirling, winning the Gran Turismo Class. John beat the class record by an hour. In addition, a 180D Mercedes Benz won the Sedan Class. It was a clean sweep for Daimler Benz.

Looking back over his racing career, Fitch thought the 1955 Mille Miglia was his greatest drive. Later, he wrote about the moment when he found out he had won his class, "For me, the moment was the kind that enhances the value of everything, large and small, making senses more acute, the grass greener, the sky bluer, thoughts more generous and friends dearer."

THE 1955 LE MANS

Although Fitch was an official member of the 1955 Mercedes Benz Racing Team, he was only assigned to drive in sports-car events. Other team members drove in Formula One.

Pierre Levegh and John Fitch talking it over before the race.

Daimler Benz assembled an all-star team to pursue the World Driving Championship (Formula One) and the World Sports Car Championship. Drivers at Le Mans included Juan Fangio teamed with Stirling Moss, Karl Kling with Andre Simon and Pierre Levegh with John Fitch.

JOHN COOPER FITCH

On the evening before the race, Pierre and his wife invited John to dine with them at their hotel. Even though John didn't speak a lot of French and Pierre didn't know any English, they somehow managed to communicate. John later recalled that he was "made to feel completely at home." In a conversation that night, Pierre remarked that he didn't think the front straight past the pits and grandstands was wide enough. "It's too narrow for these fast cars," he said, "and each time I go by it is with a feeling of unease, a feeling of being hemmed in." In addition, he didn't like sitting on the left as he was used to racing right-hand drive cars. The two agreed not to push their car for the first half of the race, conserving it and hoping to move up towards the end.

The three Le Mans cars were designated W196S, commonly called 300 SLRs. Many experts rated them the best sports cars in the World. The bodies were made from a flammable, but ultra-lightweight magnesium alloy called Elektron. This material reduced the weight of the cars and improved performance. However, they lacked disc brakes used on the D-Type Jaguars. To help the less efficient drum brakes, the Mercedes engineers devised large air brakes behind the drivers that could be raised to increase drag, thus slowing the cars.

French hero Pierre Levegh was not a regular member of the Mercedes team but Team Manager Alfred Neubauer felt it would be popular, even diplomatic, to include him. Remember, WWII ended only ten years previously. In 1952, driving solo, Levegh had led Le Mans in a French Talbot until the 23rd hour when mechanical trouble sidelined him, giving the win to Mercedes.

Here's what happened in 1955. More than 250,000 spectators lined the 8.38-mile course, which was essentially the same as it was for the first race in 1923 when the top speeds were around 60 mph. But by 1955, many cars exceeded 190 mph. In those days, safety requirements were minimal; seatbelts were not required, much less harnesses and roll bars.

The start of the 1955 24-Hours of Le Mans. Car #26 is the Lance Macklin Austin-Healey; the #19 is Stirling Moss in a 300 SLR; #20 is Levegh 300 SLR; #21 is Karl Kling in a 300 SLR; #22 is Briggs Cunninhgma in his C-6R; #25 is Tony Brooks in an Aston Martin and #30 is da Silva in a Gordini.

The race started at 4 p.m. on Saturday, June 11. Castellotti led off in a Ferrari followed by Mike Hawthorn in the D-Type Jaguar. Fangio, Kling and Levegh were the first drivers on the Mercedes team. The three 300 SLRs were slow getting off the line. At the end of the first lap, Levegh was seventh overall and leading his two teammates. On the next lap, Fangio passed Levegh and was third overall behind Hawthorn and Castellotti. The three engaged in a fierce duel with Hawthorn setting a new Le Mans lap record. By 6 p.m., Fangio had passed Hawthorn with Castellotti dropping back. Kling and Levegh were running together, almost a lap behind the two leaders.

JOHN COOPER FITCH

Karl Kling leading Pierre Levegh, both using the innovative air brakes that were fitted on the 300 SLRs.

Hawthorn and Fangio continued their duel and Mike took the lead again. In an effort to stay ahead, he had been ignoring signals to stop for fuel. Levegh was just behind Hawthorn, but a lap in arrears. Entering the pit straight, Mike had just passed Lance Macklin's slower Austin-Healey when he decided to pit at the last minute and cut in front of Lance. Macklin braked, swerving to the center of the track. He had failed to notice the rapidly approaching Levegh and second-place Fangio, both going over 150 mph.

Levegh hit the Austin-Healey, became airborne, and landed on top of an embankment with a closely-packed crowd behind it. The 300 SLR went into a somersault and disintegrated with parts flying about. Then the fuel caught fire causing the magnesium alloy to burst into flame. Workers poured on water, not knowing this would intensify the fire. In consequence, the inferno continued to burn for several hours. Officials put the death toll at 84 spectators plus Levegh. Later, others claimed the count was actually much higher.

After the accident, there was chaos in the stands opposite the pits. The inextinguishable magnesium of the 300 SLR burned even more when the firemen poured water on it.

Just before the accident, Madame Levegh invited Fitch to join her for coffee in the Mercedes trailer just behind the pit. When they heard an explosion, John told Madame Levegh, "Wait here; I'll see what's happened." Finding everything in chaos, he helped some injured gendarmes and journalists. Then he returned to the trailer. "I suppose my grim face must have told it all, for I didn't have to speak. Madame Levegh nodded slowly. 'I know, Fitch. It was Pierre. He is dead. I know he is dead.'"

Mercedes had a tradition of retiring the team when spectators or drivers were killed. Fitch thought they should, so he told Mercedes Chief Engineer Rudolf Uhlenhaut about the appalling number of deaths and injuries, recommending that the team withdraw. Uhlenhaut called Mercedes headquarters in Germany, but the decision required a vote of the directors, all of whom couldn't be immediately contacted.

A few hours later, John again urged Uhlenhaut to try again for a decision, which was finally made to withdraw. Two hours after the accident, the two 300 SLRs were called into the pits. The Fangio-Moss car was then two laps ahead of second-place Hawthorn, who went on to win. After the race, however, Mike was devastated and reduced to tears.

Stirling Moss had had his sights set on winning Le Mans and, with the 300 SLRs, he thought his chances were excellent. Besides that, he was teamed with Fangio, arguably the best driver in the world. When the team withdrew from the contest, Moss was heartbroken. He blamed the decision on John Fitch. I recall that even years later, Stirling held it against John.

There was little doubt that Hawthorn was the proximate cause of the accident. Whether or not he was the actual cause became a subject of some controversy. Some of the press claimed that he was culpable. Many years later, I became acquainted with a retired English nurse who, it turned out, was then Mike's girlfriend. She told me that at times he would become depressed when remembering. As we all know, Hawthorn went on to win the first World Driving Championship for the United Kingdom in 1958, after which, he retired. The following year he was killed in a single-car traffic accident.

The consequences of the 1955 Le Mans were and are far reaching. They have affected all of us involved with the sport and even everyone who uses a car. The American Automobile Association stopped sanctioning automotive competition. The big three U.S. auto makers—Ford, GM and Chrysler—withdrew from direct participation. Racing was banned in Switzerland. The next round of the World Championship—the Nurburgring—was cancelled, as was the Carrera Panamericana. And a great deal of attention was paid to driver and spectator protection as well as accident prevention. Another positive result was that self-taught engineer John Fitch devoted himself towards problems of safety.

On June 16, 1955, a funeral was held for Pierre Levegh in Paris. Fitch went accompanied by Stirling Moss and Mike Collins. In addition to the mourners, there was a large number of newspaper reporters as well as a throng of curiosity seekers. They created a side show that was uncalled for. After the service, Madame Levegh received a line of those who came to pay their respects. When it was Fitch's turn, he said something about his great respect for Pierre.

After Le Mans, John returned to the home near that of Rudi Caraciola he had rented in Lugano, Switzerland. His third son, Stephen, was born in July. Fitch was able to spend a lot of time with his family that summer. Although he was an official member of the Mercedes team, insofar as Formula One events were concerned, he was a reserve driver. Even though he had to be on hand for the June 19 Dutch and the July 26 British Grands Prix, he didn't drive.

THE 1955 GRAND PRIX AT MONZA

The last Formula One race in 1955 was the Grand Prix of Italy held on September 11 at Autodromo Nazionale at Monza. After the Le Mans disaster, the French, German, Swiss and Spanish Grands Prix were cancelled. So Monza was the last Formula One that year. Even though Mercedes dropped out of racing after 1955, the team still continued to contest the World Drivers' Championship that year.

Monza was only a 50 mile drive from Lugano. John practiced in a Mercedes, but their regular drivers—Juan Fangio, Piero Taruffi, Stirling Moss and Karl Kling—were on hand, so Fitch didn't make the team lineup. In addition to being on the Mercedes team, Stirling had a year-old Formula One Maserati. He always wanted it available and brought it to Monza with his crew. So Moss offered the ride to Fitch which he gratefully accepted. The car was a full season behind in development in comparison with the other Maseratis at Monza. Stirling's crew members—Alf Francis and Tony Robinson—painted the car with a blue and white stripe, U.S. colors to signify that an American would be at the wheel. Saturday's practice didn't go well for John because the Maserati engine was running rough.

In addition to the Mercedes team, there were six Ferraris and seven Maseratis, three Gordinis as well as two Vanwalls. Twenty cars started, but by the third lap, the engine in the Fitch Maserati was blowing blue smoke and throwing oil which blurred John's goggles.

At that point, it seemed doubtful that the car would be able to last much longer much less go for 50 laps. Nevertheless, he soldiered on. When all four Mercedes in a row passed, Fitch was able to tuck in behind and catch a tow due to the tunnel of air created behind a fast-moving car. On lap 32, Karl Kling dropped out with a broken gear box. He was followed by nine more who failed to finish including Stirling Moss.

John Fitch in the Stirling Moss Maserati at Monza.

When John passed his pit, he noticed a dejected Stirling standing with Francis and Robinson. During the race, Fitch made two stops to add oil and drink a cup of cold water. Each time he came into his pit, the spectators, pulling for an underdog, would cheer and wave. This encouraged John to finish. On the last lap, he was crawling along with the engine stuttering along and pouring clouds of smoke. It probably couldn't have made another lap, but Fitch took the checkered flag in ninth, four laps behind the winner: Fangio. Taruffi was second with Eugenio Castellotti third in a

Ferrari. Juan Manuel Fangio was crowned the 1955 World Driving Champion.

The Italian Grand Prix at Monza was the last time Karl Kling and John Fitch drove in a Formula One event. And it was the last Grand Prix for the Mercedes team until the 2010 Bahrain Grand Prix. The team wouldn't win another Grand Prix until 2012 in China.

THE 1955 TOURIST TROPHY

The next sports car event for the Mercedes team was the Tourist Trophy at Dundrod on September 17, 1955. It was the first race that counted for the World's Championship. The others that would normally have taken place were cancelled due to the Le Mans tragedy. That year's Tourist Trophy was its Golden Jubilee. The first event was run in 1905 on the Isle of Man. The cream of international talent was on hand.

The circuit was in Northern Ireland near the Dundrod/Belfast International Airport. It was 7.4 miles on rural public roads just west of Belfast. Treacherous, narrow and twisty, it was bordered by hedge rows, deep ditches and stone walls. Fitch wrote that "I had considered it extremely dangerous when I competed there in 1953 and found no reason in 1955 to change my opinion.

The world's best teams—Mercedes-Benz, Ferrari, Aston Martin, Jaguar and Maserati—came to Dundrod in 1955. Juan Fangio, Stirling Moss, John Fitch, Karl Kling, Andre Simon and Wolfgang von Trips were in 300SLRs. A strong Aston Martin team was led by Roy Salvadori, Peter Collins and Tony Brooks. Jaguar brought Mike Hawthorn and Desmond Titterington. Drivers for Ferrari included Piero Taruffi and Umberto Maglioli. Carroll Shelby and Masten Gregory shared a Porsche Spyder.

After two days of practice, Fitch was doing well. His lap times were even better than von Trips'. Moss had won the Tourist Trophy two previous times at Dundrod, so he undoubtedly knew the circuit better than anyone else. His times were the best of all.

JOHN COOPER FITCH

Originally, Neubauer had John with von Trips, but the day before the race, he changed the lineup putting Moss and Fitch together.

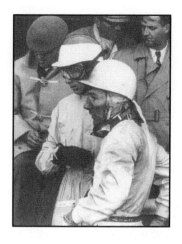

Right: John Fitch and Stirling Moss

Before the start, it had been raining, making the road slippery. After the band played *God Save the Queen,* the drivers ran across the track and jumped into their cars. Hawthorn was first away, followed by Moss. By the end of the first lap, Moss had passed Hawthorn and Fangio took over third. During the first hour, Stirling held a commanding lead with Fangio and Hawthorn dicing for second. But during the second hour, Moss had scraped a bank and blown a tire. The tread from the damaged tire whipped around and stripped away the magnesium skin. During a long pit stop, the damaged sections were removed. Stirling decided to rest, so Fitch took over.

Below: John Fitch in the 300 SLR at the 1955 Tourist Trophy.

Meanwhile, Hawthorn went into the lead. After three laps, it started to rain, harder this time. Six laps later, John came in and Moss took over again. Two laps before the finish, the Jag engine in the Hawthorn car failed and Mike had to walk back. Mercedes finished in triumph. Moss and Fitch were first, Fangio and Kling second with von Trips and Simon third. Only 27 of the 55 starters managed to go the distance and take the checkered flag.

That year's Tourist Trophy, however, was riddled with problems and tragedy. On the third lap, Jim Mayers lost control of his Cooper, crashed into a stone wall and was killed. Bill Smyth's Connaught ran into the wreckage and later died from his injuries. Richard Mainwaring in an Elva died when he overturned and was trapped in his burning car. The Dundrod circuit was abandoned and subsequent Tourist Trophies were held on purpose-built tracks in England.

THE 1955 TARGA FLORIO

Fitch returned to his temporary home at Lugano, Switzerland and spent a month with the family. The last World Manufacturers' Championship event of the season took place on the island of Sicily a month later. John flew to Palermo where he had once landed in 1943 during the war. The team was housed in the fabulous Hotel Igiea in the historic city.

The Targa Florio that year was held on October 16. It was first held in 1906 and the last in 1977. In the opinion of many who raced there, it was one of their toughest and most difficult. According to Brian Redman, who won in 1970, "One 44 mile lap had 710 cor-

ners, not to mention unforgiving poles, stone walls, dogs, spectators and farm animals. Surfaces ranged from bad to worse. A missed turn might mean a horrific drop down the side of a mountain." Some called it "The Terrible Targa." It took some competitors more than ten hours to cover the 13 laps.

The Targa was the culmination of a season-long duel between Mercedes and Ferrari. After winning the Tourist Trophy, Mercedes had 16 points while Ferrari led with 19. To take the Championship, Mercedes had to win both first and second, so Daimler-Benz launched an all-out effort.

Two weeks before the start, it was on Sicily with eight sports cars, eight trucks, 15 passenger cars and 45 mechanics. Ferrari, on the other hand and without the financial resources the Germans had, brought only three cars and six mechanics. Since they weren't in contention, Jaguar and Aston Martin didn't show.

Fitch was teamed with Desmond Titterington, Moss with close friend, Peter Collins, while Fangio was with Kling. Carroll Shelby and Gino Munaron drove one of the factory Ferraris. Maserati entered six of their new A6GCS models and independents brought two more. There was a total of 47 entrants. Moss set the fastest time in practice followed by Fangio.

The Mercedes Benz team (left to right): John Fitch, Desmond Titterington, Peter Collins, Stirling Moss, Juan Fangio and Karl Kling.

Normally, Sicily enjoys sunshine, but on this occasion, it rained so heavily the day before the race that sections of the course were damaged. The drivers were warned about this. At 7 a.m., the first car set off. They were released, smallest first, at 30-second intervals. This meant that the larger-displacement cars had a lot of passing to do. Titterington drove the first four laps and then was to be replaced by Fitch for another four and so on.

JOHN COOPER FITCH

By the end of the first lap, Stirling was leading. He had passed the entire field setting a new lap record of 44 minutes. On the third lap, Moss broke his own record. Then he went off the road on a fast curve, slid into a field and ended up straddling a huge rock without any traction for the rear wheels. With some help from nearby spectators, he was able to get back on the road.

John Fitch in the 300 SLR leading Eugenio Castellotti in a Ferrari.

Back in the pits, the car looked as if there wouldn't be sufficient time to fix it. The damaged body was jammed against the front tires and the radiator was gushing water. Amazingly, the mechanics were able to do enough to get Collins on the road after only a few minutes. At the first scheduled stop, Kling replaced Fangio and Fitch took over for Titterington who was in fourth. John was holding the position when the tail end lost traction on gravel and the left end hit a stone wall. Fitch was surprised that he was able to resume with the car seemingly in good order. Collins also hit a wall with the already damaged 300SLR, but again was able to continue after bending the fenders away from the wheels.

After nine hours, 47 minutes and 14 seconds, Stirling Moss took the checkered flag. The Fangio/Kling Mercedes was second, only three minutes later with the Costellotti/Manzon 860 Monza Ferrari in third. John Fitch and Desmond Titterington were fourth, another 13 minutes behind the winner. Daimler-Benz had done what it had to do to take the World Manufacturers' Championship away from Ferrari by finishing first as well as second. Twenty of the 47 starters managed to complete the races.

Juan Fangio won the Formula One World Drivers' Championship for Mercedes and the team won the Sports Cars and Gran Turismo titles as well on top of the Manufacturers. It was a feat never before achieved and a tribute to the engineering skill of the company. Daimler-Benz announced it was retiring from racing, wisely enough at the height of its glory. John Fitch was more than happy to have played a part.

Then it was time for the Fitch family to leave their temporary domicile in lovely Lugano and head home to Connecticut.

THE YEAR OF THE CORVETTE

In 1953, General Motors introduced the Chevrolet Corvette. Hailed by some as the long-awaited American sports car, for the most part, they were derided by "purists." It was apparent that Chevrolet had set out to create a "boulevard cruiser" rather than a serious sports car. It was powered by an anemic six-cylinder overhead-valve engine. All had an automatic transmission some called "slushomatic." In comparison with, for instance, an XK120 Jaguar, it couldn't get out of its way, particularly in terms of handling. Needless to say, it left a lot to be desired by enthusiasts.

In 1954, Chevrolet dealers received 3,640 Corvettes. But by 1955, the company was only able to sell 674 and was considering the discontinuation of the line.

John Fitch set a record in a Corvette on the sand at Daytona Beach in 1956.

Corvette Chief Engineer Zora Arkus-Duntov made improvements in 1956, replacing the engine with a 265-cid V8 along with a three-speed manual transmission. Chevrolet Chief Engineer Ed Cole asked John Fitch to run one at Daytona Beach (opposite page) where he set a new production-car Flying-Mile record of 145mph. Cole decided to enter a Corvette team in the 12-Hours of Sebring that March. But Arkus-Dutov told Cole it was impossible to field respectable racers in the time available. Still determined, Cole turned to Fitch, who accepted the assignment as team manager and lead driver.

In February and only five weeks before the race, one car was delivered to John at Sebring where he had rented a facility. According to John, the first thing he did was to drive the wheels off it. Many problems arose: oil leaked, engine mounts loosened, fan belts were thrown and the handling was inadequate. The wheels actually fell off and had to be replaced with racing wheels and tires. Another problem was that, in order to qualify for Production Class C, whatever changes Fitch made had to be options offered by the factory to dealers and their customers.

By the time the race started, the Corvettes had magnesium wheels, special brake drums, heavier sway bars, oversize gas tanks, shorter steering columns and special shock absorbers. In each instance, Fitch had to negotiate approval from Detroit. To accomplish this in the small amount of time remaining, John cultivated allies among the production-car engineers.

A month before the race, four more cars arrived, three for production Class C and one with a larger engine for modified Class B. Fitch and Walt Hansgen drove the modified car (#1) with the production cars driven by Dale Duncan and Allen Eager in #5, Ray Crawford and Max Goldman in #6 plus Ernie Erickson and Chuck Hanson in #7. All were experienced road racers. Two mechanics from the local Chevrolet dealer joined the crew during the last hectic days.

JOHN COOPER FITCH

The lineup for the start: Corvette #1 – John Fitch/Walt Hansgen, Ferrari #2 – Ruttman/Hively, Corvette #3 – Davis/Gatz (not part of the GM team), Corvette #5 – Duncan/Eager, Corvette #6 - Crawford/Goldman, Corvette #7 – Ericson/Hassan.

Just before the start on March 24, 1956, the top Chevrolet engineer, "Rosey" Rosenberger, told John that "If we stop right now and never race a Corvette, we've learned enough to justify all your efforts." The original Corvette had been transformed into a serious competitor, and in only a little longer than one month. What John Fitch had done has often been overlooked by automotive historians, who, more often than not, accord much of the credit to Zora Arkus-Duntov.

The 12-Hours of Sebring always begins with a Le Mans start. On that sunny Saturday at 10 a.m., all 60 drivers lined up in their marked spots across from their cars. John Fitch in the modified Corvette was at the head of the pack. When the flag fell, they sprinted across the ramp and jumped into the cockpits. John started off using only half throttle due to the high torque of the first gear. As he sped away, he could see the Duncan Corvette in his rearview mirror with the other two Corvettes not far behind. He knew his team was off to a good start.

Fitch's lead, however didn't last long. As John turned off the airport onto a connecting road, Mike Hawthorn in his D-Type

Jaguar slipped by. Next, just before the first straight, Stirling Moss in the Aston Martin passed. At the end of the first lap, Fitch was third overall. His next lap, however, was a different story. The clutch started to slip. So while in top gear at high revs, he rode on the clutch to burn the clutch lining. The maneuver worked because the only effect was to reduce the maximum possible revs—6,000—to 5,600. This solution wasn't great, but it was possible to continue for the duration of the race.

As John continued on, he was faced with more bad news. He saw that his Number 5 Corvette had pulled over to the side of the road. Dale Duncan was bent over an empty wheel well. Apparently the axle had broken and the car was out of the race. An hour later, John saw Corvette Number 7 moving slowly with smoke trailing from the exhaust. Now two of the four team cars were out. In order to have any sort of decent result, he knew Number 1 just had to finish, so he drove on handling it like, as he said, "A basket of eggs."

After two hours, Fitch pulled in to hand over to Walt Hansgen. When he got out of the car, he was told some more bad news. Corvette Number 6 was seizing in gear and had to proceed using only third gear. The Corvettes had three-speed transmissions, so third was the top gear. With a lot of torque, it was able to continue at least at a somewhat decent speed. The race was not even half over and the team was two down and two stumbling.

As the hours wore on, one by one, other cars came limping into their pits or broke down somewhere on the course. At 10 p.m., an aerial rocket signaled the end. At that point, however, cars were still running on the course and had yet to cross the finish line. Only 24 of the 60 starters managed to actually finish.

Fitch and Hansgen were ninth overall and won Class B, Crawford and Goldman won Class C.

JOHN COOPER FITCH

The other two failed to finish. Corvette won the Team Prize! Ed Cole had led GM where no American manufacturer had dared before: into the big league of World Championship competition. Corvettes had become true sports cars.

John Fitch driving the SS Corvette that won Class B.

From then on, and with the Fitch-developed options, Corvettes began to appear in road races. Chevrolet asked John to compete in SCCA Nationals, but he was otherwise committed and recommended Dick Thompson, who won the SCCA National Championship that year. Others who successfully raced Corvettes in 1956 included Bill Pollack, Ray Crawford, Dick Guldstrand and Jim Peterson.

LIME ROCK PARK

In 1956, John Fitch not only made a major contribution to motorsports by transforming Corvettes into serious sports cars, he was also instrumental in the design of Lime Rock Park. Starting with the previous-years tragedy at Le Mans, John became troubled regarding safety on tracks as well as on public roads. It was a concern that would last for his lifetime.

The Lime Rock Park course has been hailed as the safest in the world, largely due to the influence and contributions of John Fitch. Located in Connecticut, the site is in the extreme Northwestern corner of the state, just south of the town of Lakeville. It started out life as a sandy gravel pit. In 1955, Jim Vail was operating the pit for his father, who owned the land. Jim, and his friend Jack Fisher, who owned an MGTC, messed around in their spare time racing around the gravel pit.

Somehow some SCCA members—Briggs Cunningham and a few friends—heard what was going on and approached Vail with the idea of building a race track. He became intrigued and, after getting the approval of his father, he had an aerial photo of the 385-acre property taken. Then he went to a Lime Rock town meeting and received permission. Because the gravel pit was an operating business, there was a lot of earth-moving equipment on hand.

Vail's plan was to build a 3-mile track. But due to a hurricane and ensuing flood in the winter of 1955, part of the site was under ten feet of muddy water. The resultant delay as well as a problem with raising the necessary money jeopardized the project.

The next summer, Fitch got involved with helping to raise funds and took over as the designer. He was able to involve Bill Milliken, the head of the Vehicle Dynamics Department at the Cornell University Aeronautical Laboratory. John talked Milliken, a long-time racing friend, into using the track design as a center for the study of safety. A number of the resultant features were incorporated. The first was the addition of a 300-foot paved escape road at the end of the main straightaway. Next, Fitch included wide areas on the outside of all the turns. Soft and sandy, they dramatically slowed cars who failed to make the turn. Also, he insisted on the removal of such things as trees, boulders or anything else nearby that would damage a car on impact. His concept was, whenever a car went astray, natural features would do much to slow it down. The result has been a program of automotive research with the expectation that the findings will be applicable, not only to the sport, but also public highways.

The Lime Rock circuit is a scientifically engineered roadway laid out with the benefit of expert opinion.

From the outset, Fitch meant it to be more than just another course. As he said, "It could help us answer the question of just what happens to a car when it leaves a road, for whatever reason, and what can bring it to rest in safety for all its occupants."

Lime Rock Park is truly unique among purpose-built racing facilities. It's the oldest, continuously-operating road course in the U.S. Nothing else matches its ambiance, for it's truly a park. There are no grandstands or high-rise suite seating, but there is tremendous spectator viewing where fans can spread blankets, set out a picnic lunch and sip wine while cars whiz past.

For Fitch, safety for spectators was just as important. Fortunately, the geography was almost ideal. The infield features a large hill where more than half of the track can be seen. This means that good views are afforded while, at the same time, everyone is far from the usual dangers. From the time the track opened in 1957 and to this day, no spectator has ever been injured at Lime Rock Park. In the years to come, John would be involved with Lime Rock in a number of other ways.

THE CUNNINGHAM D-TYPES

A few months after Sebring, Fitch rejoined the Cunningham Team, this time piloting D-Type Jaguars. Briggs had given up the idea of building his own cars. For the rest of 1956, John drove in ten SCCA races plus the season-windup, the Speed Week at Nassau in the Bahamas.

Briggs Cunningham and John Fitch with one of Briggs' D-Type Jaguars.

The first was the SCCA Nationals at the Cumberland, Maryland Municipal Airport on May 20. John drove Briggs' D-Type, ending up fourth overall and second in class.

Walt Hansgen won in a D-Type, followed by Jack McAfee in a 550 Porsche Spyder and Bill Lloyd in his 300S Maserati. Next was Thompson, Connecticut on September 2-3. On Sunday, Walt won again, this time followed by John. Jaguars dominated with third-place George Constantine in another D. On Monday John placed second behind Walt, but this time John's buddy, Masten Gregory placed third in a Ferrari.

The event that fall that Fitch most remembered was at the new Road America course near Elkhart Lake, Wisconsin. The new facility had replaced the public-road courses at nearby Elkhart Lake. It was something of a homecoming because John had won the last two—1951 and 52— of the three events ever held there. He had taken the checkered flags in Briggs' Cunninghams.

John Fitch wins at Road America near Elkhart Lake.

The reason John remembered it so well was because, after Sebring, it was his most important drive in 1956. And it was one he didn't win. It was an SCCA National held on September 9, only a week after the two days of racing at Thompson.

The main event that Sunday was a six-hour enduro. It was a requirement that each entry be co-driven by its owner. Accordingly, Briggs Cunningham entered himself and John Fitch in Brigg's D-Type Jaguar.

Briggs' plan was for John to drive the first two hours, himself the next two and John to finish off. Their competition included Carroll Shelby and Sherwood Johnston in Ferraris, Paul O'Shea and Phil Hill in a 300 SL and Jim Jeffords in a Corvette.

At the flag, Fitch forged into the lead with John Kilborn's 4.5 Ferrari following. By the end of John's turn, he was within a few hundred feet of lapping Kilborn. He handed over to Briggs on the 43rd lap. During the rather long pit stop, Kilborn went in front. Cunningham rejoined in third after another D-Type.

When Briggs came in after his two-hours, he was still in third. Some necessary Jaguar engine adjustments were made and then Fitch took off after Kilborn and the D-Type. At this point, the two were a full lap ahead. So John gave it everything he had. With a half hour remaining, he passed into second, still 35 seconds behind the Ferrari. Even though he was making up about four seconds a lap, it wouldn't be enough to win. When he pushed even harder, the brakes became erratic until the left-rear locked solid, forcing John down the escape road. At the reduced speed, the brake unlocked and he got back on the course and resumed catching the leader. At the end, the Kilborn/Hively Ferrari won by seven seconds. John was sure he would have won if the race had lasted just a few laps longer.

There were two more weekends at Thompson that year for John Fitch. Both were SCCA Regionals, not Nationals, so they didn't count for the National Championship. Nevertheless, Briggs decided to enter his D-Types. The first was on October 7, the second only three weeks later.

Fitch drove in two races each day, the first a preliminary, the second the main event. On the 7th, he won both while on the 28th he was second both times to his friend, Walt Hansgen.

The final international event for 1956 was the Speed Week at Nassau. As usual, some big stars were there including Stirling Moss, the Marquis Alfonzo de Portago, Carroll Shelby, Phil Hill and Masten Gregory. John drove Cunningham's D-Type in four races. The first was the Governor's Trophy run in two heats. Shelby won the first one in John Edgar's Ferrari, followed by Fitch and Phil in another Ferrari. The second heat didn't go as well for John. He only managed a fourth behind Shelby, Portago and Lou Brero. The third for Fitch was the Jaguar Trophy which he won going away. The final race of the week was the main event, the Nassau Trophy. Unfortunately, after so much use, the Jaguar engine gave up the ghost and John posted a DNF. Stirling won it in a Maserati with Masten and Alfonzo following in Ferraris.

By the end of the 1956 season, at age 39, Fitch felt that he was becoming an "old man" in racing. In those days, only a very few top pilots were over 40. It was considered a young-man's sport. For example, Moss, who had started racing at age 20, was only 27 that year. Now, of course, things have changed. We live longer and many of us keep in shape with better diets and exercise. In 1993, Mario Andretti was still racing at age 53.

By then, John had other pursuits on his agenda. In addition, with three children at home, he had a family to raise. He didn't make very many Nationals in 1956 and ended the year placing fourth in the C-Modified Class for the SCCA National Championship. From then on, and with some notable exceptions, Fitch began to scale down in terms of driving race cars.

THE 1957 SEBRING

After the 1956 Sebring, Fitch kept in close touch with the Chevrolet Division at General Motors. Initially, this was through correspondence with Walter MacKenzie who was in charge of the company's racing program. "Mac," as he was called, reported directly to Ed Cole, who had been promoted to Chevrolet General Manager. John proposed that the company embark on a full-scale racing program, not only with production Corvettes, but also a Formula One team. Mac wrote that a "very special" Corvette was planned for the next year's Sebring.

John Fitch (left), Zora Arkus-Duntov and Mrs. Duntov at the factory.

In December, Mac called John and asked him to come to Detroit to take a look at the project. Chief Engineer Zora Arkus-Duntov met Fitch at the airport and they drove out to the plant.

When they arrived, Zora showed John the blueprints for the Corvette SS. "SS" meant supers sports; it was to be an all-out sports-racing car, presumably one capable of contesting for the World Sports Car Championship title.

To say the least, John was impressed with the plan that had been devised by Zora. It was to be powered by a 4.6-liter Chevrolet V-8 with fuel injection and aluminum heads, estimated to be capable of producing about 315 hp. The lightweight magnesium alloy body would house a steel-tubing space frame with magnesium wheels and a de Dion rear end. It was estimated to be around 1,000 pounds lighter than a production Corvette. Arkus-Duntov told Fitch they were already working on the car and that it would be ready for Sebring. To John, that seemed an impossibility since the race would take place on March 23, 1957, only three months away.

While he was in Detroit, Fitch met with Ed Cole, who was mightily impressed with what John had accomplished the previous year. Cole said that the total Sebring race operation would be in John's hands. He would manage the entire team consisting of the SS, a modified and two production Corvettes. In addition John, himself, would be one of the SS drivers. John was delighted because he thought that this would be the first chance since the Cunninghams for an American-made car to compete in international prototype racing. And unlike the previous year, Zora Arkus-Duntov was fully on board.

The original plan was to have two months for testing before the race. But this didn't happen. Work on the SS went slowly and the car wasn't ready until the beginning of March with the race only three weeks away. As before, Fitch rented space in a big hangar at Sebring. John arrived there with two months to go along with three Corvettes plus a practice SS they called the "mule." It had started life as a mockup for the SS. It had a rough-looking prototype body. With a few exceptions, it combined the mechanical components that would be incorporated into the actual SS.

JOHN COOPER FITCH

In spite of its shortcomings, the mule performed well. The first time John took it out, he was able to unofficially break the Sebring track record. After making some minor adjustments, he took it out again in practice. He wanted to see how it might stack up against the competition. So he slowed on the back straight and waited for a group of cars to come by. The group consisted of a Ferrari, a Maserati and a D-Type Jaguar. Following them for some laps, Fitch was very encouraged. When he came in, Zora was more cautious. "To win Sebring the first time out with an experimental car like ours would take more luck than it's decent to expect. There isn't that much luck in this game." Below: Fitch got a lot of attention.

As John circulated around in practice, the performance astounded and amazed onlookers, to such an extent that it produced some very favorable press. Fitch invited his former team-mates, Juan Manuel Fangio and Stirling Moss to give it a try. Fangio was able to break the previous year's record by more than two seconds.

"Fantastico," he said when he emerged from the cockpit. He remarked that he could have done a few seconds faster if he really pushed. Stirling's time was less than a second behind that of Fangio. When the real SS arrived, the GM mechanics removed the springs and shock absorbers from the mule and put them on the SS.

John had asked Piero Taruffi to come to co-drive the SS. Two months previously, he had won the Mille Miglia. At 50 years old and with a great deal of successful driving as well as engineering experience, he would be steady and reliable. Fitch assigned a number of very experienced drivers for the other three cars. The modified Corvette (#2)—dubbed the SR2—was driven by Pete Lovely and Paul O'Shea. Production car #3 had John Kilborn, Jim Jeffords and Dale Duncan while production #4 was driven by Dr. Dick Thompson and Gaston Andrey.

The SR2 was made for GM Design chief Bill Mitchell. Earlier in 1957, it had set a class Flying-Mile record on the sand at Daytona of 152 mph. The "SR" designation stood for Sebring Racer. At approximately 2,000 pounds, it was some 700 pounds lighter than production Corvettes. With an increased displacement, reworked heads and a higher compression ratio, it produced 255 bhp.

At 10 a.m. on March 23, the flag dropped and the drivers ran across the track, jumped into their cars and sped off. The SS engine was slow to fire up, so John got a rather slow start. At the end of the long straight, he passed two of the Corvettes. At the end of the first lap, he was sixth overall behind three Ferraris and two Maseratis. While trying to stay with the leading group, the brakes started pulling, first to the right and then to the left. After the third lap, John pulled into the pits. It turned out that one of the front tires had two flat spots. Both front tires were changed in a few seconds and he was off again.

The brakes, however, were still erratic. John adapted to the problem and was still able to turn rather respectable lap times, even matching those of Hawthorn's the previous year.

JOHN COOPER FITCH

But then, the engine cut out. Fortunately, he was near enough to the paddocks so he was able to coast in. After the mechanics got the engine going again, John went out again and continued even though the brakes were still bad. When the engine stopped again, John pulled over, got out the tool kit and started to work. The rules were that any repairs made on the course had to be done by the driver alone. After trying a few things, he replaced the coil and the engine came alive.   Below: Fitch in the SS.

Although Fitch resumed making competitive lap times, the engine started to overheat. The oil temperature gauge stood at 300 degrees and water was 225. The heat in the cockpit was becoming unbearable and John was soaked in perspiration. In addition, the handling got increasingly worse, to such an extent that it might cause an accident. At that point, John decided to call it a day and pulled into the pits.

"No use," John said, "I can barely keep it on the road." Fitch wanted to quit, but Ed Cole didn't agree. "We can't give up; we've come too far," he said. So he told Taruffi to take over and try to make it to the finish. After two laps, Piero came in and agreed with John's decision to quit.

Juan Fangio and Jean Behra won in a 4.5 Maserati with Stirling Moss and Harry Schell second in a 3-liter Maserati. The rest of the GM team, however, turned in a flawless performance.

John Fitch in the SS Corvette (#1) is being passed by Juan Fangio in a 450S Maserati (#19) and Stirling Moss in a 300S Maserati (#20).

The Thompson/Andrey production Corvette finished 12th overall and first in class. The Kilborn/Jeffords/Duncan production car was 15th overall and second in class. The Lovely/O'Shea SR2 was 16th overall and seventh in class. The SR2 had to run in the same class as the winning Maseratis.

The Corvette Super Sport had shown promise while it was still running. But the 1957 Sebring was its only time on a track. Dr. Dick Thompson continued racing Corvettes that year and ended up winning the SCCA National Championship. In 1958 and '59 Jim Jeffords was the SCCA National Champion at the wheel of his "Purple-People Eater" Corvette. Pete Lovely opened a Corvette-only dealership in Seattle and raced Corvettes eight or ten times in the Northwest. Corvettes were becoming more and more dominant in production road races all across the U.S., due largely to John Fitch and Zora Arkus-Duntov.

MANAGING LIME ROCK

John had a somewhat active racing schedule for the balance of 1957. All were in the U.S. with the exception of Nassau at the end of the year. Chevrolet discontinued its racing program and Mercedes Benz had done likewise in 1956. Now he had young children to bring up and a new job: managing Lime Rock Park. To be nearer, the family moved to an old house in Lakeville, Connecticut where John and Elizabeth would live for the rest of their lives.

Managing Lime Rock turned out to be his "day job." John had a lot of ideas. For one thing, he wanted to extend the course to include some high-banked turns similar to the one at Monza. He thought this would attract Champ Cars and make Lime Rock the Indy of the East. The previous year, a group of U.S. Champ Cars and Indy drivers had gone all the way to Italy to drive at Monza. For a number of reasons John's vision never was realized.

Always the innovator, Fitch organized and scheduled an endurance race for small sedans. He called it the "Little Le Mans." Originally he wanted it to be a 12 hour event, but the local police objected to night-time racing, so it was reduced to ten hours. In order to fit in between dawn and dusk, it started at 8 a.m. There were three displacement classes: A) under 750cc, B) 750-1,200cc and C) 1,200-1,600cc. Like Le Mans and Sebring, there was an "Index of Performance." The race took place on Saturday, October 19, 1957. Local law didn't (and still doesn't) allow racing on Sundays.

The race began with a Le Mans start when 31 drivers sprinted across the track and jumped into their cars. Entries included Volvos, Saabs, Nash Metropolitans, Renaults, Panhards, DKWs, VWs, Austins, Fiats and a Simca. At the start, two Volvos took the lead and battled with Charles Kolb in the Simca. Dick Thompson, who had driven a Corvette at Sebring for John, followed along in a Saab. At the ninth hour, Vernon Bennett with co-driver Ralph Schantz in a Volvo took the lead and won, averaging almost 60 mph. Volvos took the first four places overall and Saabs captured the first four Index of Performance places.

The event was unique, undoubtedly the first ever endurance race for "economy cars." It demonstrated the reliability of the breed as well as the importance of racing for sales publicity.

John Fitch was able to have a full season of events held at Lime Rock during its first year. And he drove in five of them as well. The very first race at Lime Rock was only a month after Sebring. John drove Briggs Cunningham's D-Type Jaguar, but the engine let him down and he failed to finish. Next on the Lime Rock agenda was on June 9, 1957. It was an SCCA National event and John drove the D-Type again. Carroll Shelby won the main event in John Edgar's 300S Maserati followed by Lake Underwood in a 550 Porsche Spyder and then John in third. Shelby was winning so many races in the Edgar Maserati that John wanted to give one a try. Vincent Andrus let Fitch drive his 300S on July 7 at Lime Rock. Drive he did indeed and posted only the second win John had that year. Three weeks later, there was another race there where John took the same 300S to second overall.

Even though it was his favorite, Lime Rock wasn't the only venue where Fitch raced during 1957. John drove 12 times that year including Sebring. He won at Thompson on May 28 and was second at Road America on June 23 behind Walt Hansgen, both in Briggs' D Jags.

JOHN COOPER FITCH

John Fitch at Nassau.

In December, it was back to Nassau again for the annual Speed Week. Driving the Andrus Maserati, John was second in the first heat of the Governor's Trophy race, but failed to finish the second heat. With the 300S repaired, Fitch was ready for the main event, the Nassau Memorial Trophy. A total of 57 cars started. Stirling Moss won in a 3.5 Ferrari and Richie Ginther was second in a 4.9 with John third. Among others, Masten Gregory and Phil Hill failed to finish.

Fitch ran a total of 20 races during 1957. He was first overall two times, five times second and third twice while winning nine class victories. Except for Sebring where his entrant was General Motors, all others were either for Briggs Cunningham or Vincent Andrus.

WINDING DOWN

Starting with 1952, John raced at Sebring every year with the exception of 1955 when he spent most of the time in Europe. By 1958, Briggs Cunningham had not only stopped making and racing his Cunninghams, but also had ended his Jaguar program. He entered John and Ed Hugus at Sebring in a Ferrari 250 Testa Rossa. The 1958 overall winners—Phil Hill and Peter Collins in a Ferrari 250 Testa Rossa—covered a total of 200 laps. The engine in the Fitch/Hugus Testa Rossa, however, gave up the ghost after only 85 laps.

Since he was always on hand as the General Manager, the only venue other than Sebring where Fitch raced that year was Lime Rock. First on John's agenda was a New England Championship event on April 27, 1958. John's name doesn't appear in the official program, but, since the Andrus Maserati 200S was on hand and Vincent was agreeable, Fitch made a post entry. He finished second overall and second in Class D Modified. The other two events that John entered were both SCCA Nationals, the first on June 15, the second on July 5. How Fitch persuaded the SCCA to have two Nationals at the same venue in one year, much less only three weeks apart, remains a mystery. At any rate, Walt Hansgen in Cunningham's Lister Jaguar won the June main event followed by Bob Oker in an Aston Martin DB3S and Bob Holbert in a 550RS Porsche Spyder. John was fourth in the Maserati. Ed Crawford in another Cunningham Lister Jaguar won the July main event with Walt in second and John in third.

JOHN COOPER FITCH

The construction of Lime Rock didn't end John's interest in safety innovations for racing and highways. He continued to use the facility where he was the general manager as a kind of outdoor laboratory, a testing ground for automotive safety measures. Fitch started serving as a consultant to a number of research and governmental organizations on the subject including National Technologies, DeConte Industries and Consulier Automotive. He also participated as a design consultant for other racetracks including Mosport, St. Jovite and Watkins Glen.

According to John, "The premise is that a race course can establish dependable references in the behavior of both vehicle and driver because, unlike the highway or the proving ground, it can be used to full capacity. Driver ability and effort, usually difficult variables, are relatively uniform under racing conditions. What is learned here can be applied later on public roads."

During 1958, Fitch started doing some writing. Incensed by an article, "Stop Us Before We Kill Again!," that appeared in the November 1957 edition of the *Saturday Evening Post*, that advocated outlawing auto racing, he wrote a rebuttal that was in the March 1958 edition of *The Sports Car Journal* (published and edited by Dick Sherwin and Art Evans) titled "Let's Get It Straight!." In addition, he worked on his autobiography—*Adventure On Wheels*—published the following year.

In 1959, John ran in a few more races than during the previous year. As before, however, most were at Lime Rock. The one that got the most attention was a Formula Libre event on July 25. Even though Rodger Ward was famous by then, the race many remember him for was winning in a nine-year-old Midget. Fitch remembered that race: "He blew off Fangio's World Championship 250 Maserati driven very well by Chuck Daigh, plus George Constantine in an Aston Martin, Ricardo Rodriguez in a 3-liter Maserati and me in a Cooper Monaco. Others were many of the fast cars of the day, all with very good drivers. The consensus among old-time race fans was that this was Rodger's greatest race ever."

Rodger Ward leading the pack in the Midget (#1) at Lime Rock.

On June 13, 1959, he raced a Corvette for GM Honcho Bill Mitchell at Road America in a 500 miler, but failed to finish when the brakes went out. John's best finish that year was on September 6 at Meadowdale where he was third overall and first in class driving the Cooper-Monaco. The only time he ran in a NASCAR event was at Harewood in Canada again in the Cooper. He led the race for 41 laps, but then the engine failed.

BACK TO LE MANS

Although he raced now and then until 1966, the last time Fitch was a serious competitor in important international events was in 1960 at Sebring and Le Mans. Briggs Cunningham decided to have another go at the World Sports Car Championship, this time with Corvettes. He entered himself and John in the March 28th 12-Hours of Sebring, but they failed to finish when a wheel fell off causing a minor accident.

The big daddy of the Championship was, of course, Le Mans. Cunningham entered three Corvettes plus a prototype E Jaguar. John with Bob Grossman (car #3), Dick Thompson with Fred Windridge (#2) and Bill Kimberly with Briggs (#1) piloted the Corvettes. Fitch and Grossman were a good team having often been friendly opponents.

Unlike other times with Corvettes, Fitch didn't have any duties other than to race. The Cunningham team arrived five days before the race in order to practice. Elizabeth came with John. In free time, they enjoyed touring the French countryside, shopping and indulging in the wonderful food.

Always the inventor, John devised what he called a "tachograph." It was an electronic device that recorded engine revolutions per minute. Using it, a car's performance could be analyzed, thus leading towards maximizing operation. It was one of the very first times that employed telemetry in racing. Although they had powerful engines, the Corvettes weren't seen by the so-called "experts" as serious challengers to the factory teams.

Dick Thompson is running towards Corvette #2 and John Fitch is running towards Corvette #3.

There were no qualifying races or time trials. Cars were placed in the row according to displacement. With the largest at 4.6 liters, the Cunningham Corvettes were one, two and three; hence the numbers on the cars. After the flag fell and the drivers ran across the track and jumped into their cars, with the most powerful engines, the three Corvettes led off. But that didn't last long.

A little after 6 p.m., an enormous rainstorm started. Fortunately, the Corvettes were fitted with hardtops, keeping the drivers dry. Many of the others were in roadsters and got very wet. When the rain started, Bill Kimberly had an accident when he ran off the course. Luckily Bill was not injured. Then Dick Thompson skidded into a bank, damaging the car to the extent that he couldn't continue. So within the first three hours, two of the three Cunningham Corvettes were out. This left Fitch who was running in 13th place. For some reason, John's car seemed to handle better in the wet. John said it was because the Corvette had skinny tires.

JOHN COOPER FITCH

The plan was for John to come in at 10 p.m. and Grossman to take over. But at the time, Fitch was gaining on most of the others, so he elected to continue on into the night. After passing all of the Porsches, he was able to pass Olivier Gendebien in a Ferrari who was leading. Previously, Gendebien was more than a lap ahead of John, so this put him on the same lap, although far behind. During the heaviest downpour, Fitch got up to third overall. Later, John remarked that "rain was the great equalizer and I was delighted to make the most of a huge break."

John Fitch delivered a remarkable drive at the 1960 Le Mans.

When the rain stopped and the surface dried out, the sports-racing cars started to pass the production Corvette. Towards the end, the engine started to overheat. During a pit stop, the crew packed it with ice. According to Briggs, "We knew the car would have a good finish if it could make just four more laps. Adding coolant wasn't allowed, so the space between the two banks of cylinders was filled with ice. This was repeated during another stop."

This maneuver resulted in the Fitch/Grossman Corvette finishing eighth overall and first in the GT 5000 Class. It was the best a Corvette would do at Le Mans until 2001 when they finished first and second. Fifty-five cars started the race, but only 25 were able to last for 24 hours. The Olivier Gendebien/Paul Frère Ferrari won with another Ferrari second and an Aston Martin third.

Although John Fitch continued to enter an occasional race, his remarkable drive at the 1960 Le Mans essentially marked the close of his outstanding professional career.

John was still the general manager of Lime Rock. It was a corporation with the majority of the stock held by Jim Vail. John had a minority interest. The problem was that the track wasn't making very much money and the company was near bankruptcy. The only events were SCCA races which didn't attract many spectators. John decided something had to be done, but Vail wouldn't go along with John's plans. So John contacted Jim Haynes, who had just sold his plastics company located in Lakeville. He put up the money and they bought out Vail in 1964. At this point, Haynes took over management and ran the track until 1986. Eventually, Jim was able to make it profitable. As an aside, Haynes performed the same miracle for Road America when it was failing in 1987. He put it back on its feet and was the general manager for a number of years.

THE FITCH SPRINT

In 1961, John ended his tenure as general manager at Lime Rock and founded John Fitch and Co. in nearby Falls Village, Connecticut. The company manufactured aftermarket kits for Chevrolet Corvairs. When installed, the components in the kit transformed the dowdy Corvair into a sports car capable of competing in SCCA races. He named the result the "Fitch Sprint." The 1961 Corvair Monza model had two carburetors; the kit added two more. The engine modifications increased the power from 102 to 150 bhp. In addition, the rear suspension was stiffened with new springs, shocks and an anti-sway bar.   Below: Fitch with a Sprint.

Some cosmetic trimmings gave the Sprint a distinctive appearance. John made an arrangement with General Motors whereby dealers could order a kit and install it for their customers for $427.65. The company didn't keep accurate records, but it was estimated that quite a few thousand were sold. *Car and Driver* magazine featured it in the September 1965 edition with a picture of a Sprint and all the parts on the cover. The headline was, "Corvair Sprint—Bargain GT Car."

Next, John conceived a car he called the "Phoenix." (above) It was a two-seat sports car based on the Corvair engine and transmission. He persuaded his friend, Colby Whitmore, to design the body. What Whitmore came up with is truly beautiful. It has flip-up headlights and a removable hard top. A roll bar is integrated in the design. All the other modifications and additions that had been used in the Sprint were incorporated plus front-wheel disc brakes and Weber carburetors. The Phoenix weighs only 1,950 pounds and delivers 175 bhp. It was to sell for $8,700. The prototype was displayed at Abercrombie & Fitch in New York during August 1966, resulting in some 100 eager buyers placing $500 deposits.

Then, however, insurmountable trouble arose. Ralph Nader had written a book, *Unsafe at Any Speed*, published in 1965; it became a best-seller in 1966. It was highly critical of the safety features—or lack thereof—in automobile design. Nader condemned the Corvair as "unsafe at any speed." In September 1966, the National Highway Safety Administration mandated a number of requirements be incorporated on any automobile sold in the U.S. The result was that a number of European sports cars were no longer available for purchase. In addition, General Motors discontinued the Corvair line. The result was that Fitch had to give up his plan to manufacture Phoenixes. The one prototype, however, survived and remained in John's possession for his lifetime. The saving grace, as it turned out, was that the same law that killed the Phoenix resulted in the success of the Fitch Inertial Barriers. General Motors salvaged something; the body design of the 1968 Corvette has a close similarity to the Phoenix.

In 1967, John DeLorean was running the Pontiac Division for General Motors. Aware of Fitch's transformation of the Corvair, DeLorean sent Fitch a Pontiac Firebird to play around with as an engineering exercise. Fitch did his usual magic on the Firebird. After the car was received back at Pontiac, the company lost interest and never pursued the idea. Fitch, however, continued and did perhaps as many as eight cars, but, since he was involved in a number of other projects, dropped the program.

THE LAST RACE

The Cunningham/Fitch/Jordan Porsche 904 at the 1966 Sebring.

In 1961, '62, '63, '65 and '66, Fitch drove at Sebring. In 1965 and '66, he and Briggs co-drove a Porsche 904. In 1966, they added a third co-driver: Davey Jordan. Unfortunately, they didn't finish when the engine gave up after 248 laps. This was the last time John Fitch or Briggs Cunningham drove in anger. Davey Jordan remembered that race:

> *In the first part of January, 1966 I received a hand written letter from Briggs Cunningham, inviting me to co-drive with him and John Fitch at Sebring!*

JOHN COOPER FITCH

I had met Mr. Cunningham the year before, but I had never met John Fitch. When John arrived at Sebring, I was impressed that, at 42 years of age, he was tall, slender, and impeccably dressed with slacks, sports shirt and a Tommy Bahama hat. He had a great smile and personality. Briggs was 60 years young and one of the nicest people you would ever meet.

Otto Zipper was our team manager, and he assigned me to qualify the car. On the second lap, I came up on A.J. Foyt in his Ford Mk II, just before the longest straight on the track. He had just left the pits and was warming up the car, and not up to speed yet. I tucked in behind him as close as I could, trying to get a tow down the backstretch. It worked beyond my wildest expectations. I went into the corner at the end of the straight as deep as possible with the nose of the 904 under the rear of the Mk II. When I pulled into the pits, Otto had a smirk on his face and I knew we had qualified well. It turned out to be my best job of qualifying ever; with a lap of 3:18.6, good for 25th on the grid and a new lap record for the class.

Our race strategy was straight forward. Briggs didn't push his cars to the limit and would usually finish without mechanical problems. Our race plan was not to abuse the car and bring it home for a finish. Briggs would start out, I would run the second and the last stint, taking over from Fitch in the early evening.

Briggs started the race as planned. The 904 was running like a clock. The fuel ran down and Briggs brought the car in for its first stop and driver change. I took the wheel and sped out onto the track, trying to keep consistent, yet with competitive lap times. My turn was uneventful. It was hot when I brought the car in for John to take over and I was soaking wet. Briggs was there with a cold wash cloth and instructed me to put it on the back of my neck, it felt so good. Briggs was the most considerate car owner I had ever met! The sun had set and it was time for our last stop. John was due in, but he had missed the IN signal. We didn't know if he had run out of gas or what had happened. On a course that was over 5 miles per lap, it would be easy to run out. Just as we were all getting a little panicky, John pulled into the pits, and shut the engine down. They serviced the car and I drove down the pit lane to re-enter the race. As soon as I got the green flag and floored the gas, a loud rapping noise came from the engine! I limped back to the pits. We were out; the engine had broken a valve spring. What a disappointment.

Ken Miles and Lloyd Ruby won for Ford in their Shelby American Ford X-1 Roadster. Our 904 was placed 35th with 148 laps completed. This was the last race for Briggs Cunningham and John Fitch.

THE FITCH INERTIAL BARRIER

Ever since the horrific crash at Le Mans in 1955, John Fitch was concerned with automotive safety, not only on race tracks, but also streets and highways. While he was the general manager at Lime Rock, he had continued his experimentation regarding safety that he had started with the track design and layout. He was concerned with how to stop speeding cars before their drivers sustained serious injuries and the cars badly damaged.

The problem, not only on racetracks but also highways, is how to bring a car to a relatively safe stop. Cement barriers are especially unkind to cars as well as occupants. In 1966, the National Safety Council estimated that 55,000 fatalities were caused by cars striking various fixed objects. Hay bales on race courses weren't much better. They are so low that cars often overturn when they hit them. Guardrails also cause accidents. John's solution was the ubiquitous round barrels seen everywhere. Technically, they are "Fitch Inertial Barriers."

John knew that barriers had to be tall enough so cars couldn't jump over them. He came upon the idea of using sufficiently tall barrels. His first impulse was to pack a barrel with sand. But this presents a hard object. What he ended up inventing was a plastic barrel filled with sections of sand and air. The unique barrels are made by Union Carbide. They are stiff, strong, lightweight and fracture easily. When struck by a car, the barrel disintegrates and slows the car. His first public demonstration was held on September 5, 1967 at Lime Rock.

Fitch conducted numerous tests in order to refine his design.

Further testing revealed that placing a number of Fitch barriers in a triangular arrangement was even more effective. In 1968, John formed a company—Fitch Inertial Barriers, Inc. or FIBCO—to manufacture and market his invention. Fitch kept doing demonstrations, not only at Lime Rock, but elsewhere, trying to sell barriers. At first, it was a tough sell in that there was resistance in placing what looked like trash cans on highways. Eventually, he persuaded some state and federal officials as well as the press to take a look. Finally, on November 2, 1969, the first barrier was placed on the intersection of Interstate 84 and Connecticut Highway 3. A few days later, John received a letter and a box of cigars from a man thanking Fitch for saving his life.

But even after this victory, the product wasn't flying off the shelf. What was needed was a more aggressive sales campaign. By January 1971, the company was coming close to failure. John enlisted George Crawford, who had had a track record of resurrecting enterprises. Crawford negotiated some loans, and sold stock. The company received a patent on September 20, 1971, an important factor for investors. In 1966, Congress had passed the National Traffic Motor Vehicle Act. Subsequently, the National Highway Safety Administration was established. Fitch was able to convince the administrators regarding the efficacy of his barriers and, when a state bought Fitch Inertial Barriers, the federal government supplied 90% of the funding. Thereafter, sales were steady and the company was making a healthy profit.

Today, Fitch Inertial Barriers are used on almost all highways.

John Fitch was the largest stockholder—at 30%—and Chief Executive Officer of Fitch Inertial Barriers, Inc. The company, however, was secure in the hands of George Crawford. By 1972, the company had an elegant headquarters office in Boston. That Spring, the board of directors suggested to John that if Crawford were to become the president, he would be more effective in dealing with customers and distributors. At a subsequent meeting, John refused. The board however, convinced him to become the chairman of the board instead of the CEO.

By April, Fitch found out by accident that Crawford had been keeping John from knowing much about what was going on. He confronted Crawford and they got into an unpleasant dispute. In consultation with his attorney, John learned that Crawford had taken power. Fitch initiated a proxy fight thinking that the other stockholders would side with him. Towards the end of 1973, John lost the battle.

So things continued on at FIBCO. John still retained his stock, but had no input insofar as management was concerned. Eventually, Fitch sold all his stock to the Highway Safety Design and Fabrication Corp. The company retained John as a consultant and product developer, a position he held well into the nineties.

OTHER SAFETY INNOVATIONS

The inertial barriers weren't John's only thing he invented in his pursuit of safety. Two more were what he called Compression Barriers and Displaceable Guardrails. He received patents for both. The Compression Barrier is a retrofit for oval race tracks. Many serious accidents have resulted from speeding cars hitting cement walls surrounding ovals. When struck by a car, John's invention absorbs energy by compressing. Then it redirects the car so that it continues on parallel to the wall.

The Displaceable Guardrail (above) is mounted on skids so that when struck, it slides, thus absorbing energy and slows the vehicle.

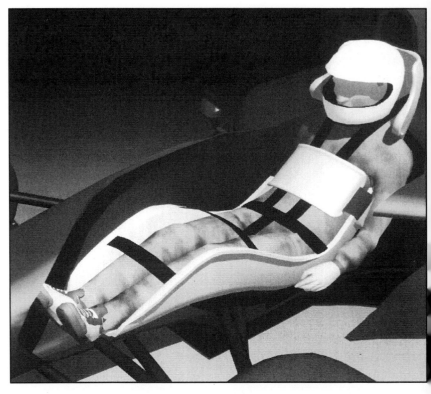

In addition, John developed the Fitch Driver Safety Capsule (above). The design is a capsule that surrounds and protects the driver from the effects of a collision while, at the same time leaving him free to steer, brake and shift gears. The sidewalls of the device protect the torso and legs. It is mounted on a track, which with the use of shear pins, progressively resists forward travel in the event of a collision. Much of what John put in his Capsule has since been incorporated in modern racecars. Spectators are often amazed when, after a horrendous-appearing accident, the driver gets out and walks away.

In 1998, John Cooper Fitch was awarded the Kenneth Stonex Award from the Transportation Research Board of the National Academy of Sciences for his lifelong contributions to safety. In presenting the award, Chairman John Carney said that "In all, John Fitch's achievements in road safety throughout the world have spanned four and a half decades. His lifetime contributions have covered the full spectrum of highway safety: the roadside, the vehicle and the driver. All have resulted in significant reductions in injuries and fatalities on the motorways of the world."

THE NEW MILLENIUM

John Fitch was inducted into the Corvette Hall of Fame in 2000 and the following year into the Sebring Hall of Fame.

In 2002, Daimler Benz hosted a 50th anniversary to celebrate the Mercedes Benz victory at the 1952 Mexican Road Race, the Carrera Panamericana. John Fitch, the only American driver on the team, was invited to take part. The plan was to drive the original route in modern Mercedes cars. In addition, they brought the 1952 300 SL coupe, driven by Herman Lang, that placed second in 1952. Along with John, Phil Hill, who placed sixth in 1952, was invited to the af-

fair. Phil had written an article about it that was published in the April 1953 edition of *Road & Track*.

The Mercedes Benz 300 SL roadster that John drove in the 1952 Carrera no longer exists. So John's friend, Bob Sirna, created an exact replica. Bob took both John and the car to Lord March's 2002 Festival of Speed at Goodwood where Fitch provided a demonstration in front of an appreciative crowd. The car is now owned by Bruce McCaw.

JOHN COOPER FITCH

Sirna also had a production Mercedes Benz 1955 300 SL Gullwing. The car represented a remembrance of the time Fitch drove the same make and model at the 1955 Mille Miglia. After 1957 when there were a number of fatalities, the Mille Miglia was abandoned as being too dangerous. From 1958 through 1961, it was changed from a race into a rally. In 1977 it was revived again as a parade called the Mille Miglia Storica. The parade, which lasts for several days, retraces the original route.

John Fitch and Bob Sirna with Bob's 300 SL in 2002 at Firenze.

In 2002, Bob took John along with the car to Italy for the event. Even though John remembered some of the route from almost 50 years ago, they spent some considerable time studying the venue before starting out. Fitch drove and Sirna was the navigator.

Bob Sirna brought his 300 SL and John Fitch to Bonneville for record attempts in 2003, 2004 and 2005.

The 2002 Storica wasn't Sirna's only project. The following year (2003), he took John and the car to Bonneville. The goal was to set a new speed record in the F/GT class for touring sports cars. The class record at that time was 168 mph set by a Datsun 240Z. Previously, Sirna had been driving his 300 SL at almost 160 mph, so he needed another 10 mph. Since the rules allowed it, Bob did a number of engine modifications plus some changes to make the car lighter.

Another friend of John, Carl Goodwin, who had been a member of the crew, reported about it in the Nov/Dec 2003 edition of *Vintage Motorsport*:

> *The car left Detroit in its trailer. It and some of the team, including the Fitch Motorsport Historian Larry Berman, arrived at Bonneville on Sunday, August 12. Tech inspection at Bonneville is a tedious process, but safety is of utmost importance. John Fitch, then 86 years old, attended the required driver orientation on Tuesday morning. He qualified as the oldest "rookie driver" in Bonneville history. By noon, we were ready to get in line for the rookie runs.*
>
> *For the first run on Wednesday, lower tire pressures were used. This made a big difference in reducing the directional instability of the car. Unfortunately, there was no time recorded on that first run. The engine, which sounded great on the starting line, went up to about 3500 rpm and then started running roughly. They towed it back to the starting line and went to work. Run number two on Wednesday was a repeat performance. The powerful-sounding engine could not rev through 4000 rpm. Fitch had to again turn off the course and coast over to the return road. Ever the optimist, Fitch exclaimed, 'We've got all afternoon to fix it.'*
>
> *Sirna labored feverishly, but the conclusion was that no more runs could be made. The big adventure was over. Far from being glum, we made jokes. And as for John Fitch, he just said, 'When are we coming back, Bob?'*

Chris Szwedo made a film—*A Gullwing At Twilight*—that documented John's record attempt. It ran on PBS and was shown at a number of gatherings.

Bob brought the car and Fitch back to Bonneville in 2004 and again in 2005. Unfortunately, the 300 SL engine didn't develop sufficient power for John to set a new record. After Bonneville each year, John continued on to California and we would get together to attend the Monterey Historics.

On August 6, 2007 it was my great honor to host John Fitch's birthday party at my home in Redondo Beach, California. He had turned 90 on the 4th. My family was almost in revolt due to the numbers who came. Davey Jordan's wife, Norma, brought the cake. Davey was John's teammate at the 1966 Sebring in Briggs Cunningham's Porsche 904. Bob Bondurant flew over from Phoenix to give John a copy of his just-published biography, *Bob Bondurant,* by Phil Henny.

Some of those who came to my home to help celebrate John's 90th birthday were (left to right): Bob Bondurant, John Fitch, Phil Hill and Dick Guldstrand.

I have never heard of a more active nonagenarian. Fitch was in Los Angeles to attend a Society of Automotive Engineers conference held in Hollywood on August 7, 2007. John and Ken Berg presented a paper: "Are We Flat-Out for Survivable Deceleration? The 1955 Crash at Le Mans—Its Impact on Racing."

Ken Berg supplied me with a copy of the paper. I have tried to summarize and pick out what I think are high points:

> *Auto racing has always been dangerous, both to participants and spectators. Death and injury is not a highly visible part of racing...until it happens. Drivers can professionally tune out natural concerns for survival. Their attitudes may have lulled those others in racing that might be expected to influence automobile and auto-racing safety—for everyone.*
>
> *Are we pushing race safety improvement as fast as possible? What are the restraints to going flat out for 'survivable deceleration?' Can the inertia that is restraining safety development be overcome to produce advances in safety as great as those occurring in mechanical and electronic technologies in automotive engineering?*
>
> *I am not happy with the progress in racing safety. It has been harder to make progress in racing safety than it was for highway safety.*
>
> *All energy absorption that mitigates impact severity is governed by Newton's Laws of Motion. They require movement or travel of the decelerated element over a distance. It is the one and only factor involved. Driver restraints, in-car cushioning and driver's bodies, being flexible, compressible and extendable—all reduce the Gs that impinge on the brain, heart and other vital areas of the body. Incredibly no one in academia or engineering seems*

to be aware of this. If they are, it has not appeared in the press to my knowledge.

My friend, USAF Colonel John Stapp, conducted deceleration tests in a 600 mph rocket sled and found 45 Gs to be the limit before the eye began to leave its socket. Mechanisms sufficiently sophisticated to exploit Newton's laws and the limit of Gs will be expensive relative to the simple means developed to date. More complex devices, such as my Displaceable Guardrail that moves on impact and my Driver Capsule with greater travel than the HANS device, are the next steps to greater driver safety. I have done more than 100 development crashes.

The response from racing bodies has been typically an expression of gratitude for my efforts, along with wishes of good luck from their attorney's office, but expressing no technical interest or support, despite the outstanding success and visibility of the Fitch Inertial Barrier on the nation's highways for almost four decades.

The weekend after John delivered the paper, he was inducted into the Motorsports Hall of Fame. And in December 2007, John Fitch received the Lindley Bothwell Lifetime Achievement Award at the annual banquet of the Fabulous Fifties at the Petersen Automotive Museum.

Fitch invented, developed and received patents not only for racing and highway safety—the Fitch Inertial Barrier, the Compression Barrier, the Displaceable Guardrails and the Driver Capsule—but also he was involved with other innovations. He participated in things such as the Evans Waterless Engine Cooling System, a propylene-glycol-based cooling system that does not require pressurization, the DeConti Brake, a liquid-cooling secondary braking system for light trucks, buses and similar vehicles. He received a patent for the Fitch Fuel Catalyst which reduces the light chain molecules in gasoline thus inhibiting oxidation and microorganism growth in fuel as well as a self-leveling automobile suspension system. Outside the field of motor vehicles, he received several patents for the Salisbury Thermo-Syphon Fireplace which uses waste heat to provide convection heating and the Fitch Cervical Spine Traction Therapy that allows freedom of movement in bed while continuing to provide tension that relieves disk pressure.

On October 24, 2008, the Petersen Automotive Museum in Los Angeles held a celebration to honor Corvettes as race cars. A large number of Corvette drivers were there, but John was the star. To help celebrate, I put together a book, *Racing With Corvettes, The Early Years*. We had a box of books hot off the press that John and I autographed for his fans.

John's dear friend (and mine), Don Klein wrote this for the 2013 Lime Rock Track Program. He titled it, "Heeeeeere's Johnny!"

I'll tell you something funny about John Fitch that most people never got to see: John Fitch. Everyone has him pegged as a serious guy, and with legitimate reason. Most of the things he's famous for are deadly serious accomplishments. There's nothing funny about shooting down an enemy plane, or being taken prisoner of war. There is no humor in being trapped in a speeding racecar as it careens off track flipping end-over-end because of a broken axle, or in witnessing the most devastating accident in motorsport history from its epicenter. Yes, John experienced all of those things and more, but he not only lived to tell, he laughed to tell.

Maybe it was his deadpan delivery, but his standard one-liner that he often used at speaking engagements always got a big laugh: "People ask me if I'm glad to be here. Why, at my age, I'm glad to be anywhere!" On one occasion, bolstered by the audience's enthusiastic reaction to that remark, he decided to embellish on it by first adding, "If I knew I was going to live this long, I would have taken better care of myself!" and then, "Just the other day my eight year old granddaughter asked me, 'Gramps you're so old, did you know Jesus?' When I asked him later if she had really said that, he grinned impishly and said, "No, I just made it up; seemed funny at the time!" And it was.

But John wasn't just funny, he was fun. His enthusiasm for life and willingness to "play" made him a great traveling companion. Here's an example: In September, 2010, John was invited to be Guest of Honor at the 60th anniversary of Elkhart Lake's Road Course, which was the precursor to Road America. He asked me to go along with him, and of course I did. Our hosts had provided a suite, which consisted of two bedrooms separated by a living room and kitchen. It was a lovely arrangement, marred only by the fact that it was fly season in Wisconsin and the annoying critters were relentless. I was in my room trying to catch up on e-mails when I heard an intermittent "Thwack, thwack, thwack" coming from the kitchen. So I looked out, and there was John, wearing his tan safari jacket, wielding a rolled up newspaper in hot pursuit of a housefly, all while chanting, "The fly must die! The fly must die!" When he saw me standing idly in the doorway, he tossed me the sports section and said, "Come on! I've been chasing him for half an hour and I think he's getting tired." But it wasn't enough that I merely help him on his search and destroy mission, he insisted that I join him in the "fly must die" rallying song as well. In the end, we got the winged menace. But to be honest, I think the hapless insect laughed itself to death at the sight — and sound — of his pursuers.

JOHN COOPER FITCH

If I had to pick my favorite story to illustrate John's unique sense of humor, it would be the time we went to Le Mans for the 50th anniversary of his victory in the number three Cunningham Corvette. Our generous host, Lance Miller, who had inherited both the Corvette and his father's dream to reunite John with it, arranged for us all to stay in a hotel not far from the track. It had a small dining room that featured a standard French breakfast buffet: croissants, fruit, yogurt, and granola; stuff like that. But they also had hard-boiled eggs, which John adored. He put two on his plate, but for some reason didn't come back to our table. After a while I went back to the buffet table to see what the problem was. He explained that he couldn't find the salt. I joined him in his search, but I couldn't find any either. After a while I spotted a small, round woman with an apron who apparently worked there, but she didn't speak English and my hand gesturing and repeating "Sel? Sel?" wasn't cutting it. So a bilingual man who was watching our dilemma unfold came to our rescue and got to the bottom of it. It seems the hotel didn't normally serve eggs, but because of the big weekend they made an exception. But unfortunately, they hadn't thought to provide salt and pepper because the normal breakfast fare —fruit and cereal and so on— didn't require it. The news infuriated John. "What?! Eggs but no salt?! Impossible!" Here it was, not even 8 a.m., and the day was already off to a bad start. The prospect of dealing with a grumpy John Fitch all day wasn't pleasant, so I decided to improvise. "It's alright, John," I told him. "I have salt in my room." "You do?" he replied. "Why?" "Because when we had sandwiches at the airport yesterday I took a few extra salt packets with me. So go sit down and I'll be right back." Thankfully, he believed me. So while John headed back to the ta-

ble, I dashed up to the room. I didn't really have any salt, but what I did have was some nasal rinse powder that I use in a device called a Netti pot. It's essentially salt, and although it has other ingredients, the directions say if you swallow some it's okay. So I grabbed a few packets, raced back downstairs and handed them to John. I watched anxiously as he cracked open an egg, peeled back the shell and sprinkled on the granules. He took a bite, paused, and delivered the verdict: "Very good." Whew… mission accomplished. But then, with every additional bite, he kept heaping on the praise, finally exclaiming, "This is the best salt I ever had! You say you got it at the airport?" I munched my salt-less egg and nodded. But then he paused, mid-bite, and said, "But we didn't have sandwiches at the airport." Busted. I suppose I could have tried to convince him otherwise, suggesting that maybe he had forgotten because of jet lag or something like that. But I had never lied to John before and I wasn't about to start then. So I explained to him about the Netti pot. He reflected on the news for a moment or two, and then looked me in the eyes and said, "So I'm eating nasal rinse?" I nodded guiltily. Then he took the last bite, swallowed, and asked enthusiastically, "Got any more for tomorrow?"

Well, there are more stories like that. But I've run out of space and I thank you for reading this far. And now you know one more thing you can add to John's long list of accomplishments: pilot, war hero, race driver, inventor, car designer, race track manager, loyal friend. And comedian.

John was in remarkable good health for most of his life, but in 2011, his physical condition started to fail and he was hospitalized a number of times. By 2012, John, still living at home, spent much of his time sleeping. A mutual friend and John's neighbor, Don Klein, visited him often. One time Don asked John if he dreamed a lot. John replied that his dreams were wonderful; he would have long and intimate talks with his dear Elizabeth, who had died in 2009.

John Fitch, Art Evans and Stirling Moss at the 2005 Monterey Historics.

A highlight for John during those last months was when Stirling and Susie Moss came to visit over Labor Day. John Cooper Fitch died peacefully at age 95 on October 31, 2012 at his home in Lakeville, Connecticut surrounded by his three sons, John, Christopher (Kip) and Stephen.

John Fitch himself wrote:

> *In looking back over past decades since those frantic days racing on public roads and at early Sebrings, I*

have no regrets. In order to participate in this intense activity, I've risked everything including life itself, being motivated by what can be described simply as the pursuit of success in what some social scientists have concluded is the only truly modern sport in this age of the automobile. It deserves that status, it seems to me, because after the bare essentials of life, the automobile is one of the most desired of possessions. It provides not only the mobility of a magic carpet, but also the satisfaction of the mastery of an obedient machine, a subject and a servant of power, speed and considerable heft.

If the machine happens to be a tactile and special pleasure to drive—as in responsive handling—it becomes a physical pleasure to boot. What then could be more appropriate to race than this ubiquitous tool of modern life: the automobile.

I have had a full life. Over the duration of my career, I have had countless rewarding experiences; I've traveled extensively, lived with my family in Europe for several years, have made literally hundreds of friends among extraordinary people, and have had many rousing battles in the finest racing machines of their day. It's been a good bargain and a good life.

JOHN COOPER FITCH

NOTES

Some years ago, I became interested in and started writing about the history of motorsports. Working with John Fitch as the author and our mutual friend, automotive journalist Don Klein, we put together an account of his time on the Mercedes Benz team. *Racing With Mercedes* was published in 2006 and has gone through two editions. Two years later, John and I co-authored *Racing Corvettes, The Early Years.* When John died, I assembled a photographic remembrance that was published in the *Sports Car Digest.* (There is no charge to see it. Go online to sportscardigest.com/johnfitch/artevans.)

An "authorized biography," *John Fitch, Racing Through Life,* by James Grinnell was published in 1993. And John, himself, wrote an autobiography—*Adventure on Wheels*—that was published rather prematurely in 1959. (John lived another 53 years.)

When John came to March AFB with the Cunningham Team in November 1953, I was there taking pictures. I shook his hand and congratulated him after his victory. During the early sixties, he came to California a number of times for one reason or another. I was employed as a cinematographer on a commercial shoot where John was the protagonist. We became friends. During that time, I had a 30-foot sailboat and, when he visited, we used to sail together.

One of those times stands out in my memory. My boat was moored at King Harbor in Redondo Beach. We decided to visit Bruce Kessler at the Marina del Rey Yacht Club, about ten miles north. After some glasses of wine at the club, we set off to return. But it was dark and, as we sailed along, dense fog enveloped us to the extent that we couldn't see farther than a few feet or so. From where we were, however, we could hear the surf on the nearby beach. I steered while John listened to the surf. If it got too loud, we might run aground; if too faint, we might become lost. So, guided by the sound of the surf, he kept calling directions to me and we returned safely.

After Steve Earle instituted the Monterey Historics at Monterey, both of us went together to quite a few. John would fly out to San Francisco, I would pick him up, and we would spend the weekend together.

John Fitch and I were dear friends for some 60 years.

ACKNOWLEDGMENTS

A number of wonderful folks helped with this book. First of all, John's close friend, Don Klein, provided not only input, but also editorial suggestions. Larry Berman has documented each and every one of the events entered by Fitch including the dates, locations, entrants, cars and results. This was invaluable in keeping the chronology accurate. John Dixon researched various matters having to do with history. Ginny Dixon reviewed various drafts and corrected spelling and grammatical errors. Bob Sirna has provided input regarding his association with Fitch as has Carl Goodwin. Steve Johnson was a big help when I was challenged by my computer. In addition, John himself, went over and, after I made some changes, approved of much of what I have written.

It took me quite a while to compile this book. Fortunately, our dear friend, Carroll Shelby, was able to read much of it before he left us. I'm honored that he gave me the quote on the book cover. Almost all of the photos are from John Fitch's collection that is maintained with great care and dedication by Bob Sirna. Thank you, Bob. Other photos are from my own collection.

I took this portrait of John on January 18, 1992. The occasion was Briggs Cunninhman's 85th birthday. A number of Briggs' friends had organized the celebration. The party took place at Brigg's home near San Diego. John had come all the way from Connecticut. There was quite a crowd including Augie Pabst, Sherwood Johnson, John and Ginny Dixon, Dan and Evie Gurney, Max Balchowsky, Ginny Sims, Bill Devin and Skip Hudson.

ART EVANS, the author

Art Evans started to road race during the fifties. His first was in an MG at Palm Springs in 1955. Soon he acquired an MG Special and then a succession of XK120 Jaguars that he raced in Southern California. At the end of the decade, he campaigned the first Devin SS.

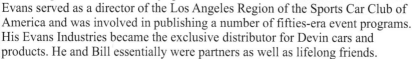

During the fifties, he and his partner, OCee Ritch, had a public relations and advertising company that represented the MG Mitten Co., Devin Enterprises, Gough Industries and other car-related organizations.

Photo by Will Edgar

Evans and another partner, Richard Sherwin, published the monthly *Sports Car Journal.* Evans served as a director of the Los Angeles Region of the Sports Car Club of America and was involved in publishing a number of fifties-era event programs. His Evans Industries became the exclusive distributor for Devin cars and products. He and Bill essentially were partners as well as lifelong friends.

Art Evans taught for a year in middle school, a year in high school and was the Chair of the Photography Department at Orange Coast College for six years. Then, a career directing and producing motion pictures for ten years followed at Paramount Pictures.

A cinematographer, Art worked on commercials that featured Mario Andretti and John Fitch. His still photographs have been displayed in numerous exhibitions including a solo at Lincoln Center in New York. Art has taken portraits of racing personalities, among many others Sir Stirling Moss, Sir Jack Brabham, Bobby Unser, Phil Hill, Dan Gurney, Carroll Shelby and John Fitch; a number have been published in various magazines and books.

Evans is the author of a number of books about motorsports. He started with a series about road racing during the fifties. Then *Ken Miles*, the only biography of that great driver. Next was another series recounting the histories of road races at California venues: Pebble Beach, Golden Gate, Paramount Ranch and Torrey Pines. Art wrote two books about Carroll Shelby: *Shelby, the Race Driver* and *The Shelby American Story.* He also co-authored books— *Racing With Mercedes* and *Racing Corvette, the Early Years*—with John Fitch. His articles have appeared in such periodicals as *AutoWeek, Vintage Motorsport, Victory Lane, Vintage Racecar, Vintage Oval Racing* and the *Sports Car Digest.*

During the eighties, Art began driving in vintage races. In 1985, he promoted a revival of the old Palm Springs Road Races followed by a succession of other events including a vintage section at the Pikes Peak Hill Climb and open-road racing in Mexico.

The Evans family lives in Redondo Beach, California. In retirement Art pursues pastimes including writing about mororsports and serving as the secretary and newsletter editor of The Fabulous Fifties Association.

Also by Art Evans

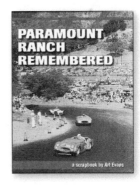

Available from:

Enthusiast Books

1-800-289-3504

www.enthusiastbooks.com